ABOUT THE AUTHOR

Paul Hurley runs Handface.co.uk, one of the UK's leading viral content companies.

Before this he was Head of Programming for Sky Box Office, Europe's first digital pay-per-view film service - and a forerunner of Netflix - as well as an entertainment executive at Yahoo! and a couple of entertainment start-ups.

Since setting up Handface, his company's content has been seen and shared all over the world – the chances are high that you've seen one of its videos, and the odds are that you've shared one. Have a look at www.handface.co.uk to see if you recognise any.

PRAISE FOR HANDFACE VIDEOS AND CONTENT:

'Viral video experts' BBC Radio 2

'Taking the internet by storm' London Metro

'Proving a hit on YouTube' Sydney Morning Herald

'Must see video' Daily Mirror

'Clever human beings…super funny and absolutely wonderful'
Screen Crush

'Hilarious' Daily Mail

'Icons of trash culture' El Pais

'Brilliant' Digital Spy

'Parodies the world both needs and deserves' The AV Club

'Great job, internet!' MoviesNos

'Very clever' Joe.ie

'Stirring' Espn.com

'Hilarious…very clever' The Huffington Post

'The intertextual translations…are a form of special reworking'
The Routledge Companion to Remix Studies

'Divertente!' Movielicious

INTRODUCTION

SOCIAL VIDEO: A video that is shared organically, on a social network or messaging service.

'Just how do I make my video go viral?'

'When is the best time to send out my video?'

'Surely there must be some secret sauce to making a viral video?'

These are questions I hear and read a lot. Which surprises me, as it's 2016 and not 2008. In 2008 I didn't know much about making viral videos and it's safe to say that not many companies did either. But time and again I still see the same patterns and am asked the same questions. And as my company, Handface Productions, is in the business of making videos and content that is targeted at going viral, and the product we've worked on has had tens of millions of views and shares, I thought I would write down what we have learned over the last few years.

As a result, this book is intended for anyone who *makes* or *commissions* videos, and anyone who is interested in the phenomenon of viral videos. It's broadly broken down into three sections. There's a lot about *method,* answering questions such as the ones at the top of the page. Then there are some personal *stories,* usually focussing on things that have happened to my company and me over the last few years. These will be presented as anecdotes, with little takeaway lessons at the end of each one. Finally there are a number of *interviews* with leading players in the field: from fellow video-makers to video commissioners.

My company, Handface Productions, makes all sorts of videos and content: we make comedy virals for clients such as The Huffington Post and Yahoo!, but we also have a more traditional corporate side, which makes everything from health videos for the National Health Service, to charity videos and government communication videos. If you like what you read and would like to discuss how we could help you, then email me at paul@handface.co.uk, or tweet me at @HandfaceVideo.

Paul Hurley, April 2016

WHY YOU NEED VIDEO

Because without it, you're not in the game.

If you don't have content that changes as your company changes, and that you can consistently send out to your customers or clients, then you are going to be a static company. And static companies get left behind. You need to be across all of the current and future social networks, and for that you are going to need content.

Think about these figures from an Invesp report in 2013 about Social Media and business, which is still very relevant going into 2016:

- All Internet users spend over a quarter of their time on the internet on social networks.
- By 2015, 'the social businessplace' was worth $30 billion.

So – if you want to be part of that $30bn businessplace, you need to be in the same place as your potential customers or clients. The social world. *Their* world. Talking *their* language. And as well as your products and services, you are going to need to provide them with what they like so that they can create an affinity with you and trust you. And what do people like on the internet? Information. Games. Funny things. And yes, cats. Funny cats.

And watching videos.

So they need to be watching *your* video.

There are some more interesting statistics in the same report.

- 87% of companies have a presence on Facebook and Twitter, with over 50% having a presence on YouTube.

If you are in the remaining 13% that don't have a social presence then stop reading right now, put down this book and go and make amends. But if you are in the big fat 87% of companies who have a social network presence, what are you doing to stand out? What content are you providing that makes you different from your competitors? And how can you create videos that will make you a market leader?

IF YOU DON'T THINK YOUTUBE IS STILL COOL, THINK AGAIN

In June of 2015, a report by GlobalWebIndex looked at which social networks were considered the 'coolest' by teens. Facebook came third, with 14% of teens citing it as the coolest site (we'll discuss Facebook and video in some depth over the course of the book. It's worth noting that looking at *all* of the respondents, Facebook placed first). Facebook-owned Instagram came second with 16% (and Instagram has implemented video in the last year with a good deal of success). Top of the class in 2015 was YouTube with 20% of all teens citing it as the 'coolest' social network.

Why is this important to you? It's simple: teens think YouTube is cool. Teens love watching videos on YouTube. In a few years these same teens will be finishing college, starting their first jobs and have disposable income ready to spend. They'll still be watching videos on YouTube (and Facebook and Instagram and plenty of other places, some of which we don't know about yet). If you're a brand, they'll be potential customers. If you make videos, they'll be potential viewers. So – to repeat what we said earlier: whose videos do you want them to be watching?

THE SHINING SWEDED, or HOW WE GOT STARTED

Sometimes you see the fully-finished product in the blink of an eye. Call it some form of fully developed iconoclastic thought, a Gladwellian gut instinct or just plain luck. But whatever it is, I had it the moment I set my eyes on the 'Sweded films' competition in 2008. Not only did I know exactly what I was going to do, on a frame-by-frame basis, but I was fairly confident we were going to give it a good shot.

We gave it a good shot. Six weeks later it took us to Hollywood.

It was February 2008. The French film director Michel Gondry (whose films include Eternal Sunshine of the Spotless Mind and The Science of Sleep) had a new film coming out called Be Kind Rewind. In the film, Jack Black plays a video store clerk who accidentally erases all of the content on his VHS tapes. Faced with a crisis, he decides to re-enact all of the films and record them onto tape, hoping to rent them out to his unwitting customers. He goes about making his own low-budget versions of Ghostbusters and Rush Hour 2 and the like. Recreating short films like this would come to be known as 'sweding', and it's a phenomenon that still exists to this day. YouTube has plenty of Sweded films.

Gondry's film distributors decided to create a competition. The rules were simple: recreate a classic film at home, with no budget or copyrighted music, and make it no longer than 2 minutes.

This sounded like fun to me, so I borrowed my sister-in-law's home video camera (a fairly sleek and useful piece of kit, but one that already seems archaic since it needed *actual tape*.) I had a location (our house), a cast of friends with myself as the deranged

Jack Nicholson character and my fiancée (now wife) Lisa as Wendy, and a weekend to do it in. If you look on YouTube for the Shining Sweded you will see the results. It's the one with the screengrab of Lisa as Shelley Duvall desperately clutching onto the knife in the bathroom as Jack's axe comes through the door.

After we edited it – on Microsoft MovieMaker (you've got to start somewhere) – we submitted it and forgot all about it. Or at least we didn't give it that much thought. At first, it had a tiny number of views on the dedicated YouTube channel for the competition, barely 3 figures, although we were getting messages on our page that people who watched it liked it. They really liked it. We liked it too, and while there were other good entries for the competition (by now hundreds of people had submitted), ours certainly felt like it had a shot.

And then we received an email to say we had won the competition. Not only was the prize significant (a trip to LA, cash, some home TV equipment and a mentor from the British film industry to help us on future projects), but the effect on viewing figures was huge. The video broke four figures over the following weekend, which at that point was heady for us.

Then it broke five figures. Then it hit 100,000. It led to all sorts of opportunities: interviews on the BBC and with the New York Times. A record label took note and a couple of months later we were directing our first pop video with a budget of over £20,000. All thanks to a zero-budget short we had made.

So what were the lessons from the Shining Sweded?

You don't need money to get views. A good idea can be enough.

But be warned - artificially 'inducing' humorous videos such as 'Charlie Bit My Finger' is easier said than done. Plenty of people have tried to create fake humorous videos: but audiences are more and more discerning in their ability to spot a fake. I'll discuss 'fake' videos in greater detail later on.

When you go YouTube the first thing you are likely to see is a screen grab of a video. If you submit a video, YouTube will now give you the chance to pick from one of three screengrabs to represent your video. This is critical – always ensure that you choose the most enticing image. When we made The Shining Sweded, we were very lucky – the choice of three did not exist. Whatever mechanic they used, it chose the frozen frame of Lisa as the image that would represent the clip. It's a very good representation of the Shelley Duvall bathroom moment in the real film, and, I think, really helped push the video. Whatever service you are using to host your video, you want to give it the best shot to stand out.

And having a platform is a huge boost. It's not just enough to put the video on YouTube. We were lucky enough that the video was perceived as good enough to spend some time on the YouTube front page. We'll discuss platforms, and how to manipulate them to your own advantage, in greater depth later.

WHAT THIS BOOK IS ABOUT, AND WHAT IT ISN'T ABOUT

There are two broad schools of thought about online video:

Organic viral videos, which people share naturally and which promote a service, product, cause or organisation.

Or *paid promotion,* which people are forced to see whether they like it or not. This might be at the start of a YouTube video they are trying to view, on Facebook, or on a random website due to the fact that they have been retargeted by advertisers for having the temerity to look something up earlier.

I'm not saying there is no place for paid-for, promoted videos. There is. And it can really help a business. There are some amazing resources out there which will teach you how to do this – and there are return on investment results which back it up.

But what we make at Handface are *organic viral* videos in the purest sense. Videos that are shared naturally – millions and millions of times over - by real people in real environments. No false counts or screwing with the view numbers. I'm not saying it's always better in every single case, but we believe it creates a better relationship between company and viewer.

That's what this book is about.

TEN MISTAKES COMPANIES MAKE WHEN CREATING VIDEOS, *or* HOW TO TELL IF YOUR VIDEO IS GOING TO BE DISASTROUS

1. Having a 'Let's make a viral!' attitude.

People in companies still say this.

In 2016.

This might be ok if we were still in 2008, but the reality hasn't dawned for a lot of companies who still blindly hire someone to 'make a viral!' The phrase seems to imply that by its very nature – just making the video - the viral will succeed, and that's a big problem. (Defining 'success' is something we will look at later on).

There are no guarantees in the video viral business, just as there are no guarantees in the film business – if there were, everyone would be producing hit films and retiring off the proceeds all the time. Companies would be much better off saying 'Let's *attempt* to make a viral, but first let's develop a strategy for how that viral might work and how we might deal with the results'. Which leads to

2. Not having a strategy.

No video is the be-all and end-all answer to a company's problems – whether it be a viral, an overview video or just a good old-fashioned ad. A video can help in lots of ways, and I believe that nearly every type of company should be considering using videos – but the video needs to be part of a bigger picture. And for that, you need a strategy. If you don't have a strategy related to your video – from its conception to its implementation – then you really need to think about whether you want to spend the money on the video in the first place. Having no plan and ignoring the basics like this can be a crucial error at this early stage.

3. Everyone drinks the Kool-Aid...*or* 'Failing to admit that your video isn't any good'.

Later in the book we'll see examples of high profile companies who have made expensive online videos and then spent an awful lot of money trying to get them promoted and seen, without anyone in the organisation having the guts to turn around and say 'Actually, this isn't that great'. It's possible to spot during the process if a video is going askew, and we will look at examples of how to do that a little later.

4. Bad feedback.

Videos are often seen by organisations as 'cool' projects to work on. Because of this, a lot of people like to get involved in the feedback loop, which can often lead to contrary feedback for the video maker. Bad feedback ruins many a potentially good video, as does...

5. Feedback governed by fear

In hierarchical institutions, which let's face it encompasses just about every single business out there, everyone has a habit of looking after their own back. The most efficient way of doing this is to please the boss, and often that boss is governed by a sense of conservatism – to shareholders, clients, the board of directors etc. This fear often trickles down and can lead to videos which play it too safe. And because of this we get a...

6. Failure to take risks.

You don't have to reinvent the wheel, but you do need to realise that it is a competitive market out there. Just look at the TV ads which clamour for our attention and need to constantly reinvent themselves in order to get it. The same is happening with online videos: the market is becoming increasingly crowded, and unless you are going to try and do something different then your chances of standing out will remain slim.

7. It's about the product, not about you, *Or* 'The curse of the start-ups'.

So many start-up videos get bogged down in telling their own story: how the founders spotted a 'problem' and how they moved heaven and earth to solve it. This is usually presented using colourful graphics. It probably makes the founders feel happy, and possibly their friends and family, but how does it lure or sell anything to a potential customer?

8. Having a confusing video.

This is often another trait of start-up videos, but it does happen to videos from larger, established companies as well. They try to redefine one of the basic rules of advertising (use one message in your ad and use it well) by cramming in everything and the kitchen sink into their video.

9. Making silly mistakes

These can range from not checking that your video is mobile compatible, not having subtitles where they are necessary (or the wrong kind of subtitles). Silly mistakes do happen and can be avoided. But only if you fall into the trap of...

10. Not devoting enough resources to the video

This doesn't just mean in terms of actual spend on the video budget, but having someone in-house who can devote enough time to the project to ensure that it is as good as it possibly can be. And liaising constantly with whoever is making the video in order to make sure the strategy always remains in focus.

I will elaborate on these themes throughout the course of the book.

WHO IS YOUR VIDEO AIMED AT?

Part of the problem of having the 'Let's make a viral!' attitude is that it is usually accompanied by a lack of consideration as to who the video is aimed at. Of course the notion of getting millions of views is commonly seen as the golden target: but is it really the be-all and end-all? Who, *exactly*, do you want to watch your videos?

A successful video strategy is essential for any campaign, and a good way of figuring out how your video might have most impact is to storyboard the path of the video. What does your ideal viewer look like, for example? Are they existing customers? New ones? What do they already think and feel about your company or service? Do they share their opinion about you? Would you *like* them to share their opinion about you?

The more you can relate to your *ideal* viewer/existing or potential customer, then the more likely you are to have success. Trying to please a huge, varied and international market can be an expensive and sometimes futile experience. Instead, by creating really good content with one person in mind, and by having a really good execution plan, you will stand more of a chance of making video content that people will empathise with.

WHAT HAPPENS IF YOUR VIDEO IS A HIT?

In early 2015, we released two videos in the space of six days that had a combined total number of views of seven figures. What this meant for us was a huge amount of press coverage, happy clients, and a lot of warm leads for our business – among the people who shared them were marketers, digital specialists and communications managers: exactly the sort of people we want to talk to about doing new business together.

What should you do if your video goes viral? Firstly, in order to actually know that it is getting out there, you should be tracking its progress closely (a simple way of doing this is to set up some keyword searches on Twitter or Hootsuite so that you can register the amounts of shares. This is a good companion to simply measuring views on YouTube, as it allows you to look at sentiment as well as pure figures. And there are also a number of services which will let you measure both sentiment and statistics).

Secondly, be ready to capitalise on it. If 100 people have shared your video, it's not too onerous a task to look up who they are and see how they might help you in the future. Or how you might help them. They could be potential long-term clients, customers, or advocates. Social video success can give you a massive amount of warm leads to exploit. You could target people and offer them discounts or early bird deals on new promotions. You could create a giant database of leads for a future campaign. You could choose the most likely candidates and turn them into brand advocates. There are so many things that you can do with all of these new fans that a key idea underpins them: be prepared. Figure out in advance what you will do with the publicity and benefits from a success, and be ready to implement that strategy once it happens.

AUTUMN 2014: LEGAL CHANGES FOR VIDEO SPOOFS, MASH-UPS, AND PARODIES

In the UK in the Autumn of 2014, a remarkable thing happened. The previously unregulated world of internet video spoofing suddenly made the news: the laws of the land were changed. Instead of coming down on the side of content owners, the decision was seen as a victory for anyone wanting to use existing material in a parody video. As long as there is no defamation or libel, it is now (in the UK and Europe at least – we will come to how this affects the situation in the US) legally acceptable to take some original video content, and create something 'new' with it, as long as the intention is to parody it.

It's worth looking at a specific paragraph from the 'Exceptions to Copyright' publication issued by the Intellectual Property Office in October 2014:

'The law is changing to allow people to use limited amounts of another's material without the owner's permission. For example, a comedian may use a few lines from a film or song for a parody sketch; a cartoonist may reference a well-known artwork or illustration for a caricature; an artist may use small fragments from a range of films to compose a larger pastiche artwork.

It is important to understand, however, that this change in the law only permits use for the purposes of caricatures, parody or pastiches to the extent that it is "fair dealing"'.

Of course, some questions remain. What is the definition of 'a short piece of original content'? What is "fair dealing"? Could someone take a whole song and make their own version of it? Does it just mean a verse, or a chorus? And regarding original filmed material, can someone take 60 seconds? Or just 30 seconds? What about sports events? As we will see, the likes of the International Olympic Committee and FIFA own the rights to very expensive sporting events, and they have been consistently tough in protecting them (any spoof using football, for example, stands a high chance of being taken down very quickly).

According to the reading of the new law, final opinion on any legal implications in a matter involving a video parody will be decided by a judge. Making him or her laugh might help the video-maker. Being involved in anything approaching libel or defamation certainly won't.

We'll look at copyright in a lot more detail, and how it is deemed to operate in the US, with example cases from Psy, The Beastie Boys and others. But next, an interview with one of the UK's foremost legal experts on the matter of copyright law, in order to examine these changes in greater detail.

INTERVIEW: DR ELEONORA ROSATI

An Italian-qualified lawyer (with experience in the area of copyright, trademarks and internet law), Eleonora Rosati is a lecturer in intellectual property (IP) law at the University of Southampton, a guest lecturer in copyright law at EDHEC Business School, and the Deputy Editor of the <u>Journal of Intellectual Property Law & Practice</u> (Oxford University Press). She also runs her own copyright law and policy consultancy (<u>e-LAWnora</u>). Previously she was a Post-Doctoral Legal Research Associate at the University of Cambridge, and worked in the IP departments of Bird&Bird LLP in Milan and London.

Q: *What was the impetus for the exception to the copyright law in September 2014?*

ER: The UK Government introduced a new exception for parody, caricature and pastiche following the recommendations contained in the 2011 Hargreaves Review of Intellectual Property and Growth and (before this) the 2006 Gowers Review of Intellectual Property. The basic idea was twofold: (1) to take fuller advantage of the possibilities offered under European Union copyright law (Directive 2001/29/EC allows Member States of the European Union to introduce an exception to copyright for parody, caricature and pastiche into their own national laws); and (2) the "need to protect the right to mock the high and mighty", as IP Minister, Baroness Neville-Rolfe pointed out.

PH: If there's a better phrase than the 'need to protect the right to mock the high and mighty' in this book, then I won't have written it. It's such a lovely expression and one which feels quintessentially British. But at its heart there is also a serious meaning: humour can be used as a weapon in a democracy as a check or balance. Of course, it's essential not to go over the top and stray into any area of danger, such as defamation of character or anything libellous or anything which will result in legal troubles. That's why, as a rule, our own work steers clear of people's private lives: we still believe that people have a right to personal privacy. But mocking the high and mighty has been a democratic tradition for a number of centuries, and it's a treat to see it written down in black and white.

Q: How can someone assess whether the amount of work used in a parody is 'reasonable and appropriate'? Ultimately, is this to be decided on a case-by-case basis?

ER: The key concept in this respect is 'fair dealing': it will be possible to use other people's works for the purpose of parody, caricature and pastiche, but any taking must be 'fair'. Fair dealing is a concept that has been developed through case law and involves - amongst others - an assessment of the amount and quality of what has been taken; what use of the earlier work has been made; and the effects of the use on the market for the original work. Yes, ultimately whether a certain use can be considered fair is determined on a case-by-case basis.

PH: It's very important to bear in mind this concept of 'fair dealing', especially in regard to the amount of original material you may be using in creating a spoof or parody.

Q: Could someone now make a parody sports video using clips of football (FIFA/UEFA/Premier league) or clips from the International Olympics Committee, for example?

ER: In principle, yes, but in doing so other IP issues might arise, for instance possible trade mark infringements, especially if the parody at hand is exploited commercially.

PH: *For many online video parodists, sport (especially football) is a very elusive subject matter. Funny videos are made, put on the internet, but takedown notices are issued almost immediately. Maybe this new ruling will help to soften the attitude of sports ruling bodies. (See also the section on Psy and FIFA).*

Q: Is it really practical that a judge could decide what is 'funny'? (And will they need help in assessing it?)

ER: What a judge will be required to do is not really to determine whether a parody is actually funny, but whether instead the author of the alleged parody wished to pursue a humorous intent.

PH: *Yet in order to understand the humorous intent, the judge will need to know the context. We see frequent stories in the press about out-of-touch judges who don't grasp the mores of contemporary society. Will they all be able to grab the nuances of Instagram or Snapchat? Is there a small business idea in educating judges on what's hot and what's not?*

Q: Does the new exception create any new issues/go far enough? Could it give video makers too much freedom?

ER: The new UK exception is fairly narrow (for instance, it leaves unaffected the laws on libel, slander and the regulation of copyright moral rights), so I do not think that it grants too much freedom.

PH: *This isn't surprising. It's also fair enough: I don't think anyone is asking for libel laws to be changed so that someone can make a funny video. But it is important to remember that these laws very much apply.*

Q: Finally, given that the internet is relatively stateless, could it

mean that what is acceptable in the UK could be seen as incriminating in another country?

ER: Yes, potentially what is acceptable as a parody in a certain country may be considered an infringement of copyright in another. In the context of potential litigation, it will be thus important to identify what the applicable law is. This is ultimately a matter of international private law.

PH: This is especially important for any multi-national organisations. Not only do they have to take local cultural sensitivities into consideration, but the laws of the land where the video is being played will also need to be recognised.

WHAT PSY CAN TEACH FIFA

Psy, the Korean rapper/singer, became one of the biggest stars of 2012 with his song 'Gangnam Style'. It's since become the first video with over 1 billion and then 2 billion views on YouTube and he became a much-loved international star (for a while at least). The video for the track, brightly lit, crisply shot and addictively weird, spawned countless tributes, the better ones themselves having millions of views (we were probably about 200th in the queue of Gangnam 'tribute acts' with our video and we still had a very impressive tally of hits).

It also represented a watershed in terms of online video and copyright. Instead of coming after anyone who used his music, parodied his video ideas or tried to out-Psy him for oddness, the Korean did a very unusual, and very revolutionary, thing. Psy released the rights to his video and his song to the world. 'If you want to play with it, then play with it', was his basic attitude. The parodists went wild. By the end of the year, Psy was one of the most famous performers in the world.

Contrast this with the practices of UEFA and FIFA, the governing bodies of world and European football. Have you seen many football virals recently? People do make them, they do get out there but you have to be lucky to see them. UEFA and FIFA have spiders crawling all over the internet to seek out copyright infringements and to issue takedown notices. I had personal experience of this in 2010 when a video I made about the World Cup started hitting an upward trend with six figure views in 24 hours and articles about it in India and Australia. But then it was gone, another amusing football video consigned to the YouTube deleted dump. Not to mention a black mark against my YouTube account – if you get enough of them you risk having your account suspended.

UEFA and FIFA undoubtedly have commitments to sponsors, a brand to protect, and a fortune in TV deals to bank. But the point is this: Psy made a simple decision and it helped him massively to become famous and well-liked. UEFA and FIFA do not have the same public perception. In fact, one could argue that it is far from it. They probably spend millions on whatever their view of social marketing is, but if they just lightened up in one small area, allowed people to make viral videos using their content, then they would have more goodwill than money can buy.

The Psy and FIFA examples also underline how videos now cross borders far more effortlessly than conventional media, which represents a radically new opportunity for companies to get their message across to new audiences and in a new way.

INTERVIEW: CASSETTEBOY

Cassetteboy is one of the leading viral video makers in the UK. You've undoubtedly seen their work (which is described below). It's hugely distinctive, very funny, and highly anticipated. 'Cassetteboy vs The Bloody Apprentice', for example, has had over 5 million views alone. As with the other interviews in the book, I asked some questions and will make some comments after each question.

Q: How would you describe your style of video?

CB: I like to call them cut and paste videos, because we cut up the original source material and paste it back together in a different order. Most people call these 'mash ups' now, but I'm less keen on that, for several (trivial) reasons. 1) I first became aware of the term Mash Up when it was applied to songs which combine the instrumental of one song with the acappella of another, and I still associate the term with mashing several disparate elements into one piece. That doesn't really describe our videos, which generally are each made from one specific source, e.g. BBC News. 2) Cassetteboy have been working together for nearly 20 years, so our work was around long before the term Mash Up became popular. 3) Our videos are created by hours of meticulous and painstaking work, and mashing is something crude that you do to a potato.

Other people seem to call these types of video YouTube Poops, but I'll be damned if I'm going to compare my work to a poop. That's for other people to do. However, these types of labels really don't matter, which makes me wonder why I've just written so much about them. In terms of describing the content of the videos, I usually go for "Silly, satirical and scatological". At least two of those applies to each specific video, if not all three.

PH: Terminology: Cassetteboy doesn't call his video mash-ups. And rightly so. I have been in several meetings where such terms are bandied about by people trying to prove they are 'in the know'. If you are going to talk detail, then know your terminology.

Q: How did you get started making the videos you make?

CB: There are two of us in Cassetteboy. We began by making compilation cassette tapes for our friends, with a minute or so of a piece of music, then a snippet of speech from the radio or TV, then another song. As we made more and more of these tapes, the bits in between the songs became more elaborate. Eventually we started to make our own music, and these compilation tapes became albums – we released 5 between 2002 and 2008.

After the albums had run their course creatively, we decided to pack it all in. We thought that we could teach ourselves video editing and maybe get some paid work out of it. We did a couple of Cassetteboy-style videos just to learn the software, and stuck them on YouTube for the hell of it. The second one, Nigella's XXXmas, got quarter of a million views before it was taken down. So we decided it might be worth doing a few more. The next one was The Bloody Apprentice, which turned out to be our most popular.

We've still had very little paid work out of it, mind you.

PH: Craft: Never underestimate the amount of time it takes to make even the most simple looking video. Cassetteboy's works are massive, time-consuming, and utterly brilliant as a result of the devotion and skill involved.

New ways of thinking: If Cassetteboy had walked into a meeting with a potential client at the start of their video career and explained what they were going to do with their 'cut and paste' video, would anyone have taken them seriously? Sometimes you have to take a leap of faith with the creative person you have hired.

Q: How do you pick your subjects?

CB: Above all else we need material that contains a wide, or at least interesting, vocabulary. If someone doesn't say anything very interesting, or doesn't express themselves in an interesting way, there's not much for us to work with. So TV shows which cover lots of different stories are ideal – like the news, or The Apprentice, which will talk about a huge range of things because of the different tasks every week.

Aside from that, we tend to pick either people we like, people we hate, or just whatever is zeitgeisty.

Q: How long does each one take to make?

It varies enormously depending on the type or amount of source material used. Let's just say a very long time. We spend at least as long tinkering with the final video, swapping a word here, changing the order there, as we do gathering the material in the first place. The Bloody Apprentice contains material from 46 episodes of the show, so that one really did take forever.

Q: What have been the main things you have learned about 'viral' videos along the way?

CB: You can never predict what's going to be a hit.

However, the most successful videos are made by people who just want to please themselves. Anyone who sets out to make a viral video is doomed to failure. Anyone who thinks they might as well share this little creative thing they've been working on may end up with a million views.

PH: "You can never predict what's going to be a hit".

William Goldman, the Hollywood screenwriter, famously wrote in his memoir 'Adventures in the Screen Trade' that 'Nobody Knows Anything'. As I mention elsewhere, even Hollywood - with its massive marketing machine, teams of skilled promotional specialists – can't always guarantee what will work at the box office. The same applies thirty years after Goldman wrote his memorable maxim, except this time the screen is much smaller. We can have the best creative, the best team working on something and the best marketing plan, but we still can't completely guarantee success. You might want to think twice about hiring anyone who 'guarantees' you a smash. Bear in mind again what Cassetteboy says: 'Anyone who sets out to make a viral video is doomed to failure. Anyone who thinks they might as well share this little creative thing they've been working on may end up with a million views'.

Q: Have you tried/do you try other styles with differing degrees of success?

CB: Yes. We made a rap video with our long time collaborator DJ Rubbish. Artistically, I think it was quite successful, but it wasn't that popular. Once you get a following I think people tend to expect more of the same, and I would be hesitant now about putting a video on our channel that deviates too much from the established Cassetteboy style.

However, we miss doing albums. Every YouTube video needs to be a single, and I miss the chance to do album tracks, and expand what we do over a longer running time. We did release a 12-minute video which was an attempt at that sort of thing, but the extended format doesn't really work on YouTube. You wouldn't want to eat a 12-course banquet in McDonalds, and you don't really want to watch a 12-minute video on YouTube.

Q: Has the success of the videos helped you in any specific way in terms of your 'career'? Have you worked with any companies for example, or do you monetize your videos in any way?

CB: No, we don't monetize our videos. We can't, as we have copyright strikes against our channel. We have had some paid work, making videos for other people, but nowhere near enough for us both to live on.

We have worked with a TV production company, trying to get a Cassetteboy TV show. We made a couple of pilots, one of which I still think was brilliant, but it didn't get picked up. And now no one will ever see it. Nearly twenty years on, Cassetteboy remains an incredibly time-consuming and labour-intensive hobby.

Q: You use a lot of material that might well be seen as 'copyright' of someone else. What is your view on how video/filmmakers use such material?

I don't really think about what anyone else does. But I think as long as you're creative with it, where's the harm? The internet has made copyright infringement unstoppable so there's no point in worrying about it.

PH: Copyright: Cassetteboy's view that 'the internet haS made copyright infringement unstoppable so there's no point in worrying about it' is important. This is the view of a leading viral-maker. Different people and companies have different opinions, but the opinion on copyright is clearly changing, as we have seen with the Autumn 2014 change in the law in the UK.

YOUTUBE

There can be few success stories in the history of the internet as impressive and unusual as YouTube. It was an overnight success on its debut in 2005 and it has risen to be consistently at the top of the most-viewed websites on a daily basis. Competition has come and gone. In the past sites such as Revver and Metacafe attempted, but ultimately failed, to move in on its territory, and while today sites such as Vevo (now owned by YouTube), Vimeo and Dailymotion have carved their own successful niches, they are just that: niches. YouTube remains the absolute monarch of online video. Any taint of a scandal (its acquisition by Google, payment rates to contributors or any other occasional legal wrangle that gets reported) is quickly forgotten as people flock to it in huge numbers. Its simple userface, immediacy (apart from its pre-roll ads) and purity attract viewers in the billions.

And it's not going anywhere.

YouTube's ongoing popularity with 18-34-year-olds is a significant reason why companies need to have a presence there, as well as being a huge opportunity for video creators. If you can stand out from the crowd (and it is insanely crowded with lots of other people trying to do exactly the same thing) then you can win new customers and fans.

But the idea of a 'one-hit' viral video which will convert viewers into lifelong supporters of your brand may be on the wane. Sure, viewers still want viral videos, but they are savvy enough to appreciate them for what they are: one-offs. A huge hit for your video may have an immediate effect on perception and marketing, but it's how you deal with it that will really make the difference. Younger audiences with increasing purchasing power want engagement, and engagement means an ongoing source of entertainment and information. YouTube's own quarterly brand reports, in which they speak directly to brands about what the Millennial crowd is watching and how they are watching it, is full of emphasis on the need for a continual stream of content. (Needless to say, YouTube is somewhat bound to say this, as it encourages brand participation on their site. But they do have a point).

The June 2014 YouTube Insights For Brands report had some other YouTube facts regarding its audience which underlines its dominance:

-   18-34 year-olds are *four* times more likely to consume video on YouTube than on any other platform.
-   The top 500 brands all grew their YouTube average monthly views in 2013.
-   Users are much *less* likely to multi-task when they are using Youtube compared to, for example, watching television.
-   YouTube is now regarded as much more of an influencer when it comes to purchasing than television.

For this last reason alone, YouTube needs to play a central role in your social video strategy.

From a video maker's point of view, YouTube really is a *social* network. Some of the most successful YouTubers, with millions of subscribers, make a consistent point of appearing in each other's videos. There is no isolation as there is in a standard television channel system, where stars are locked in so-called handcuff deals, and can only appear in certain approved programmes or on certain channels. On YouTube, it's all about sharing. The platform itself wouldn't really work if nobody shared anything. If nobody made any comments, or even didn't bother to give a thumbs up or down to a video, it would be a less immersive experience. And the makers themselves are more than aware of this, hence the cross-pollination of programming. It's an important factor to remember when devising a YouTube strategy: you don't just want to get it seen, you need to get it shared, and if you are in it for the long-term you need to get other voices of authority on YouTube giving you their own thumbs up.

What this means for brands is that having popular YouTube figures work on their videos brings some sort of guaranteed audience. But this needs to be thought about carefully: the famous YouTube personality needs to be the right fit, and it might even on occasion be more appropriate to hire someone who has a specialised following of 20,000 viewers in your specific niche rather than spending a lot more to acquire the approval of a YouTube personality with 2 million viewers, few of whom will be interested in your product. The other advantage of working with someone with 20,000 YouTube fans is that you can afford to work with more than one – the rough cost for 10 YouTubers with 20,000 fans each might work out as the same as just hiring one person with 2 million fans. If the campaign with the person with 2 million fans fails, then all the money has been wasted. But using ten spokespeople (who will ideally be genuinely excited by and keen to promote your product) should have a higher success rate, and the smaller network of fans will more than likely be happier to share what they have discovered. In summary, using a YouTube star to promote your product is often a worthwhile idea, but make sure it is the right star (at the right price) and don't purely be swayed by the number of followers that they have.

This can be especially important for anyone who is trying to raise money for a potential web series. As well as a killer idea for the show itself, the more hard facts that a series producer can present to investors or brands the better: so casting popular YouTube celebrities with thousands of followers can add bona fide credence to your project in terms of its potential audience and advertising revenue.

Another recent trend in video marketing has been what some studies refer to as 'trackvertising'. This is when brands link up with music stars and 'co-release' a new song, which is itself usually attached to a cause and in turn a product. Activia did this in 2014 with the Colombian pop star Shakira, who released her new single 'La-La-La' in support of countries in crisis along with the support of the World Food Programme. It had millions of views and shares, largely thanks to a well-handled campaign, a good song, and the millions of fans that Shakira brought to the table. But it's a risky business that could go wrong for many reasons (not least viewer scepticism) and one which requires deep pockets to fund.

WHAT TYPE OF VIDEO SHOULD YOU MAKE?

The only limit to the type of video you might consider making is the limit of your imagination, or the imagination of whoever is creating the video for you. Over the last five years we've made a whole range of videos for different companies and organisations at different times. These have included: overview videos, comedy videos, spoof TV show videos, campaign videos, charity appeal videos, health information videos, interview/vox pop videos, internal communications videos, animations, nostalgia series, infographics, music videos and so on.

Once you have figured out the purpose of your video – let's say it's a product overview video – then you need to start thinking about the production process, and your budget. Is it to be a one-off video, highlighting the benefits of your company or your service, or are you planning a campaign? Will you be making 100s of product videos for different lines that you sell? If it's the latter, how can you make this as cost-effective as possible while still retaining production values and a level of customer interest? (We'll look at product videos in greater depth later on in one of our interviews).

One area that medium to larger companies are becoming more interested in is 'Social TV'. This is essentially an extension of what many companies are already doing on Facebook and Twitter: where they have decided to employ a member of staff (or a third party) to interact directly with customers. With a Twitter feed, for example, customers can complain about or praise the benefits of a service and the Twitter representative of the company will contact them to either try and resolve their situation or retweet the praise.

Running Twitter feeds has itself become a business now, with several companies and agencies receiving fees for doing just this. A natural extension therefore is the idea of a filmed video response: let's say you run the Social Media department of a national delivery service. You receive a Tweet complaining that a package has not arrived or has gone missing. Instead of just trying to placate your customer through a series of tweets that will probably do more to irk than calm them, you could send out your rapid reaction video team to film exactly why there has been a breakdown in service. Within several hours of the complaint you have a short video explaining exactly what the specific problem was , why it happened and how you are resolving it. This could work for any company which has ventured into communicating directly with their customers on Twitter. It not only shows that you take their complaint very seriously, but you will probably impress upon them the fact that you take your role in their lives very seriously. The end result is not just one happy customer, but with the right video it can turn other current and potential customers on to your service, as well as giving you valuable filmed assets for your video archive. This type of video can work across a massive range of companies.

HOW MUCH IS IT GOING TO COST ME TO MAKE A VIDEO? *or* THE $64,000 QUESTION

The number one question that any client for a video or short film asks, and *should* ask, is 'How much is this all going to cost?' It's the right question to ask – just as in any other business transaction, it's essential to get the figures straight before commissioning any work. There are several ways of looking at it.

How much budget do you have?

If you run the marketing or communications department of a large international business, which advertises widely across TV, then you will probably be aware that high-end TV production is not cheap. Online video can be a lot cheaper, but increasingly online viewers are expecting higher-end production values. However if you are spending seven figures a year across all of your marketing, then you should be thinking about spending a proportion of that in the online video space, at least in the five-figure area.

However, if you are a one-man band and these sorts of figures are out of your reach then you are going to have to whittle down your plans to something more conservative. There are plenty of production companies out there for all budgets – and just as with any trade or service, it's highly advisable to talk to several of them, get a feel for what they might provide, and get some quotes.

What are you trying to do?

If you are trying to launch someone to the edge of space, return him or her back to earth while all the time filming the project for a live online broadcast, then obviously your spend is going to be massive. This is what Red Bull famously did in 2012 (more on this later). It's not known exactly how much Red Bull spent on the stunt, but Baumgartner's balloon alone was estimated to cost $250,000. Some commentators even reckoned that Red Bull gained about $100m worth of publicity worldwide from the event. But they are a $5bn company.

Be realistic about what you might want to achieve.

Ask for a detailed budget

If you're spending money on a video, it's essential that you should get a detailed breakdown of the budget before you commission any job. Every company will charge different amounts for different aspects of the job. I've seen cameramen charging daily rates of between £150 and £1,000, and editors from £150 to £500 per day. And don't forget the myriad other things involved in creating decent video: pre-production (someone has to plan all of this), art direction (the 'look'), costume, travel, catering, technology (cameras, hard drives etc). Sound is also a much overlooked element that makes a big difference. The costs can soon mount up, so it's essential that you meet with your video service provider and understand just how much they intend to charge and why. There are always deals to be made, particularly if you are likely to provide ongoing business to a company, so don't be afraid to negotiate.

If you're a producer dealing with a company who may be commissioning video for the first time, the budget can also help you to educate the client on some of the intricacies of the project, and show them exactly how budgets can soon mount up.

But once you have commissioned a job, don't become a *scope-pusher*. This is when someone commissions a piece of work for £2,500, yet expects it to look like it cost £250,000. Good film production companies will always strive to make their videos look as good as possible, and to push the budget as much as possible in order to provide you with the best possible service. But you need to be realistic about what is achievable for the price you are willing to pay.

If you are part of a company that is looking to create video on an ongoing basis – say a number of videos over the course of a year, for example – you'll also need to factor in staff costs. This is more than just the budget of the video, as it will encompass the time taken by your in-house member of staff who is dealing with your video producer, as well as any in-house legal costs incurred by the need to give the video the ok for release. These extra aspects of creating video can soon mount up in terms of time, and since time is money, it becomes easy to see why companies get to a point of creating their own in-house production teams.

Many companies expect a quick reward from any sort of social media activity. It doesn't always work that way. There are bound to be a few missteps, the learning curve is often steep, and success may not be quite as instant as might have been imagined. This can equally happen with video as it can with a Twitter strategy, but with video the budgets can be considerably more. This is why it is strongly advised not to look for the instant hit, but instead to think of it as a long game: one in which you will need to find your feet, your voice, and, with everything correctly in place, your audience.

YOU'VE MADE YOUR VIDEO – NOW WHAT?

Imagine spending a decent chunk of your annual marketing budget on a film that gets fewer than 100 views. It happens more often than you think.

Too often businesses want to create video content but have very little idea of how to deploy it. They think the video will stand alone as a piece of marketing that will solve all of their problems (back to the 'Let's make a viral!' attitude again). Often they just 'put it out there' and scratch their heads when it receives little response. YouTube is littered with company video channels whose video views barely break three figures.

This is not always the case – the correct method is to have the video as part of an overall campaign – but it is still astonishing to me how many companies don't think through the basics. And yes, that is still the case going into 2016. Your video, or videos, should be part of a bigger plan of how you are going run your company's communications over the next 18 months to two years. They must fit in with any other marketing you are doing. People must look at them and at least see some continuity with your other branding, even if that's as simple as just putting your current logo in the corner.

There are simple ways of getting the most out of your video. Make some noise about it before you make it or launch it. Tell your Facebook friends and Twitter followers that you are making a film. Announce the release date. Leak some stills from the shoot. Try and get any fans or advocates interested and doing some of this work on your behalf.

Don't forget that the job isn't over when the video is made. For example, you've got an amazing free marketing tool in Twitter. Who are the movers and shakers in your industry? The important bloggers? Might they be interested in retweeting it?

The creation and distribution aspects of a video's life cycle are key parts of good, strong content provision, yet surprisingly often marketing departments just focus on the 'creation'. This is especially true of content that is made for the internet and social networks: a lot of good-quality content remains unseen as the creators simply haven't done the work to spread the message.

In terms of video, some simple procedures can help to increase its viral impact:

- Send it to your brand advocates. These can be your loyal or most active followers or fans. Consider giving them a sneak peek at the video: this will give them a sense of occasion and pride, and encourage them to share the video.
- Work out a masterlist of everyone who might be interested in your video and send it to them. This could be other leading voices in your field, celebrities, or anyone who is in your video or has a tangential connection to it.
- Try as much as possible to connect with people individually. Viewers will automatically react far more positively if they feel they are being contacted personally. The sharing rates for videos will increase enormously if users are contacted in this way.
- One of the biggest mistakes to make is to just put the video out and do nothing else. It shows lack of forethought. Sure, occasionally a video will just be 'picked up', but most of the time a good deal of effort needs to be put in to make the video be seen, given that it is now a hugely competitive

market place. Some marketers will complain that lack of budget will prevent this, or that they need to devote assets to focus on larger, traditional media campaigns. This is wrong: as having spent a certain amount on the development and creation of the video, it is a waste not to devote a relatively small amount to promote it.

- Find platforms that will host your video. The bigger the platform, the better, but don't be afraid to start small. Are there localised or niche websites that are likely to be interested in what your video has to say? Who could act as a starting point for you? There are all sorts of reciprocal content-sharing deals that can be done. Ideally you want to parlay this up to having your video hosted on sites that have a bigger and better reach.

Your distribution plan needs to be rock solid. There's even a growing trend in 2016 for companies to focus as much time, effort and money on distribution as there is on creating the content in the first place.

MEASURING VIEWS ON YOUTUBE

In 2014, YouTube introduced real-time analytics for videos, and for anyone who wants to track the immediate statistics on how many people are watching their video, it's an essential part of the tracking process. The initial launch allowed users to look at views from their last five published videos in two different ways: a minute-by-minute look at views from the last hour, as well as an hour-by-hour look at views from the last 48 hours. Doubtless the analytics will expand to allow ever more in-depth looks at views on all videos, but for now it's a key tool in assessing immediate impact. It will only be a matter of time before it will be possible to track the individual boost given to a video's views by releasing a video on a certain social network at a certain time of day or night, or in a different geographical location.

MAKE SURE YOU BUDGET FOR PROMOTION

As part of your overall viral video budget: be it $1k, $5k or $50k, a company needs to make sure that it not only has a viable plan for marketing it, but also an amount of money put aside for this purpose. I would usually advocate that at least 5-10% of the budget for each video needs to be spent on promotion. It doesn't need to cost very much, as most of the tools and methods available are largely free.

The number of videos that just get released by companies expecting the world to rapturously receive them, only to fall flat, is very large. As I have discussed, the assumption that a video will go viral – even a good video that may indeed deserve to go viral – is often so ingrained in marketing departments that they forget the basics of promotion. This need not be the case: and hiring a tech-savvy graduate (or using the equivalent in your company) is often a very good way of pushing out the video.

The ability to use Twitter as a search tool is often overlooked: there are thousands of people out there who would be willing to allow you to insert themselves in the conversation about the topic of your video – as long as you approach it in the right manner. So it's worth finding your most enthusiastic, social network-savvy employee and giving them the task of online seeding and promotion. But equally important is the need to oversee what they are doing, to ensure that they are using the right tone of voice that will match both your video and your company.

Of course, you can take promotion much more seriously and enter the world of paid promotion on a social network. This has become prevalent on both Facebook and Twitter. It's not really possible to use Twitter without seeing a 'paid promotion' tweet on there.

Since Twitter has also unveiled 'native' video, whereby users can view a video in their stream with just one tap, many brands have taken advantage of this service. Because of its real-time nature and the ability to search all messages at any time to see what people are speaking about, this offers advertisers a great chance to send out what seems like bespoke advertising: you might be tweeting about a subject and suddenly a relevant ad will appear in your timeline.

While this is great from Twitter's point-of-view, it does have a drawback in that it appears akin to the intrusive advertising that has become so much of a bugbear to people in the last couple of years. This is the phenomenon whereby online shoppers will suddenly see ads for whatever they may have been browsing for on different sites. It's clever, yes, but the backlash against it, both on the web in general and also since Facebook started delivering 'targeted' ads, has been notable. It also eerily brings to mind the invasive notion of 'spying' that government agencies have been accused of in the last couple of years. But there is a hidden benefit from an advertiser's point-of-view: if they create a paid ad that is so strong that users then start to share or retweet it, other users may not know this: the ancillary views and shares may in fact outweigh the number gained by the actual paid promotion itself.

WHEN IS THE BEST TIME TO POST A VIDEO?

You need to pay careful attention to when to send out your video in order for it to be picked up/forwarded/retweeted. Midnight in your country would probably be a bad time (unless you are doing a time-specific promotion). In terms of high traffic response, typically you want to pick a spot between mid-morning and mid-afternoon between Monday to Wednesday: which allows people to settle into their working weeks, respond to any emails or crises and have that five minutes when they can scan their social or business networks for something that will entertain or educate, or ideally both.

Of course, if you are targeting an international audience, be aware of their time zones. Mondays to Wednesdays are generally better than Thursday and Friday – by the end of the week people are not only focussing on the weekend, but the early part of the week works best due to the fact that people are more receptive and more likely to share.

And it's essential to consider posting your videos multiple times: not so many that you will start to annoy any Facebook or Twitter followers, but just so that you make sure that everyone has a chance of seeing it. It's quite common practice for companies to post content multiple times, and done correctly it will not alienate your audience. People are online at different times on social networks and you want to give them as much of a chance as possible to see your work. Of course, if the video does go viral then the ideal is that everyone sees it as it is so popular, but you need to help it along. And unless you are dealing with very specific time-sensitive topics in your video, it's a good idea to think about creating something that will have 'legs' as well as shareability – in other words it should be a video that you can put out periodically, and not just serve as a one-off. You've spent a lot of time and effort making it, so make sure you maximise your return on it.

IS YOUR YOUTUBE CHANNEL SAD AND LONELY?

One of the saddest things I come across – and far more frequently than you might think – is the 'sad and lonely' YouTube channel. Once upon a time this was a YouTube channel full of hope. Its owner was planning to fill it with lots of videos, and the plan was that lots of people would come and watch them.

But that never happened. Maybe the videos weren't that good. Maybe the owner never promoted them. Or they decided to focus on another project. Or maybe the owner left and a new owner came but the new owner didn't want anything to do with the old owner or any of his projects and so completely ignored the channel. So now, several months later, all the channel consists of is a few ageing videos with fewer than 100 views each.

Sound familiar? What kind of impression does this give to a potential customer? What if that potential customer looks at a competitor's channel and see lots of up-to-date videos? Who does he or she think is the more active and engaged company? And if they are so slapdash about their YouTube channel, are they equally carefree in other aspects of their business?

There's really little excuse for not maintaining your YouTube channel. Plus it's like running your own mini TV channel. Doesn't that sound like fun?

WHAT ABOUT THOSE CONVERSION RATES?

It's a pretty simple but often overlooked idea that everyone who is making an online video for their company should have a plan. What is the video actually for? Are you trying to persuade viewers to complete a call-to-action? Are you trying to highlight the benefits of a new product? Or are you trying to simply introduce your start-up to the world? (All too often companies try to do all three and more, incorrectly in my opinion). Once you've come up with the plan, you'll be prepared to ask your budding digital agency/creative consultancy/filmmaker the question that is likely to make them flinch. It will be a very slight flinch, so be prepared to look hard for it when you ask:

'So, what sort of conversion rate are we looking at with this film'?

(By conversion rates, we generally mean the amount of people who will respond - by buying/liking/retweeting etc - to a video. Usually this is expressed as a percentage, so a 10% conversion rate would mean that 10% of the viewers would respond according to your wishes and take some form of action).

When this question was first asked, back in the Dark Ages of online video (let's say 2005), nobody knew. There was no evidence to back up any answer, so it was the equivalent of sticking a finger in the air to see which way the wind was blowing. Have things changed? In a way, both yes and no. There is still a lot of guesswork involved in predicting conversion rates. We can also track clicks. There is also a lot more statistical evidence available. However, despite having all of the theoretical and statistical information available, there is no guarantee that a viral will fly according to your hopes.

It can also be a dangerous business to predict conversion rates. Not just because they retain an inevitable amount of uncertainty, but also because once you drill down into the typical customer path to purchase/liking/recommendation, you will see that it is actually quite a difficult process to measure. The consumer can take a number of potential conversion routes, and your video needs to be part of an integrated strategy and plan to convert them. Is your video likely to be the *only* thing that will convert a customer? Maybe, but it is just as likely to be a peer recommendation or through awareness generated by a larger marketing campaign.

HACKGATE THE MOVIE

It was August 2011. A Sunday morning. About 11.30. I was in bed, sitting up with my laptop perched on my legs. I'd had a late night finishing my latest video and wanted to get it out there. It was a fake movie trailer about the phone-tapping scandal that was engulfing the News of the World. I needed someone to look at the video before I released it, to confirm that it was actually any good and that there weren't any obvious mistakes. I quickly looked on my Skype to see who was online. Luckily my friend Matt was. He knew my previous work. I sent him a private link to the video and he replied that he loved it.

At the same time I noticed that that the MP Tom Watson had just tweeted. This was my moment. Watson – a key figure in the huge, all-encompassing story that was the Hacking scandal – was part of my film. I had included him intentionally. If my tactics paid off, he would like it, feel a sense of satisfaction at being involved, and he would retweet it. Everyone who had an interest in the fall of the house of Murdoch was following him, and that included all of the press. I quickly made the link public, tweeted it to Watson, along with an innocent comment 'Look who's playing you in the film of the Hacking Scandal'. (I had 'cast' Peter Kay in the role. Had I thought more about it I might have chosen Nick Frost, but let's let bygones be bygones). And sure enough, on this otherwise typical and uneventful Sunday morning, Watson immediately retweeted it.

90 minutes later it was on the front of the online editions of both the Telegraph and the Guardian.

By the following morning it was the most shared video on Twitter and Facebook. It was a top trender in places like New York and South America.

On Tuesday I did an interview about it with 'El Pais', the leading Spanish newspaper. In the article they called us 'icons of trash culture'. Not the greatest accolade of all time, but it's still on the front of our website.

On Wednesday, my mother phoned me to say she had seen the video on the Lorraine Kelly breakfast show, the UK's top-rated breakfast TV show. Apparently Lorraine loved it, and my mother's joy made her son very happy.

It had thousands of views, then hundreds of thousands. And what were the lessons I took away from it in terms of making viral videos and creating new business? There were two:

Firstly, it may not have happened without Watson. If he hadn't been online at that time and taken the time to look at it then it might have remained small-scale in terms of its popularity. But I had planned all the time for that to happen. He was in it for a reason. He was one of the keys to its success.

Secondly, the thousands and thousands of people who retweeted it were the greatest example of lead generation I had ever had. All of these people had seen my work, and told their friends about it. And I could see on their Twitter profiles who they were. There were marketing managers, communication directors galore, and plenty of people with the scope to commission short videos. We printed off thousands and thousands of names and profiles and set about the time-consuming – but extremely worthwhile – job of contacting anyone of interest.

(We had success around that time with more than one 'fake film trailer' video. I discuss our 'Los 33' video later. But as soon as I felt we had exploited one theme, or type of video, we moved on to find a new format. I don't want to be pigeonholed as the company that just makes one 'type' of video).

INTERVIEW – JON SALMON

Jon Salmon is the former Head of Video at London's Seven, spearheading the award-winning content marketing agency's continued drive into cross-platform video content. A consultant on digital video, connected TV and broadcast projects for the British Film Institute, Universal Music, GlaxoSmithKline and AOL, Jon was formerly Head of Video and Internet TV at TalkTalk and has 15 years' experience across web and broadcast video.

Q:What do you think the important technical developments might be in the next ten years in terms of online video?

JS: Ten years ago I was working on my first live webcast from a posh boardroom overlooking the Thames with Joan Collins. The webcast was a weekly event called 'LineOne Live' with a host of celebrities to promote the launch of a new portal and subscription-free 56k dial-up service – yes a full 56k!

Video has experienced a phenomenal pace of technological change and will continue to evolve rapidly during the next ten years in ways that we are yet to even imagine. An ever increasing proliferation of devices, including Smartphones, tablets, PCs, TVs, Set-Top Boxes and game consoles and associated operating systems, are coming onto the market all the time. Manufacturers are already developing the next phase of how we will consume video, including Ultra High-definition TV (UHDTV) and H.265 codecs.

Storage - Back in 1965 Intel co-founder Gordon E. Moore stated that the number of components on integrated circuits had doubled every year over the previous five years. Moore's Law is now attributed to a number of technical predictions and the same can be said for the cost of storage.

Encoding video into multiple formats creates additional storage requirements and therefore increased operational costs. Adding a new encoding format for a platform or device would have required detailed forecasting to make sure the additional overhead and storage costs were cost-effective. Historically this has been a real barrier for content owners wanting to digitise existing content and reach emerging platforms and new audiences.

Amazon and Google, however, are now dramatically reducing the cost of encoding and hosting video content with the launch of cloud-based services. While a number of other providers are offering similar services, it will be the competitive nature between these two online goliaths that makes it a certainty the price for hosting and delivering video will just keep on falling. This will make it easier for new entrants to deliver great video content to an ever-increasing variety of devices.

And those new entrants won't necessarily be the next YouTube phenomenon, celebrities or global brands investing in content but could actually be your daughter or son Lifecasting a continual broadcast from a pair of connected glasses, capturing every moment using wearable technology. While this may sound slightly farfetched, we now have the first generation of teenagers who don't know a life before the Internet and where the sharing of what was previously personal information is now commonplace. We can only assume that the next generation of teenagers will be even more comfortable at sharing their life online and digitally storing this information remotely on servers.

Speed – The increased availability of online content is directly linked to enhanced connectivity making it easier and quicker to watch video over the internet. Superfast broadband is not only accessible at home but now in your hands with the launch of 4G mobile networks, where downloading a TV show takes just a matter of seconds.

Viewer expectations are now at an all-time high where they expect on-demand and want to watch TV whenever, wherever and however they want. The increased connectivity within towns and cities will see a dramatic rise in the popularity of viewing sites showing video, especially while on the move using your mobile.

While broadcasters have initially lead the way at providing services like the BBC iPlayer and Channel 4's catch-up service, they will have an increasing challenge for viewers' eyeballs with more nimble entrants producing and distributing content direct to the viewer.

One area where broadcasters and film studios can potentially fight back is with the investment in higher picture and sound quality. Ultra High-definition TV (UHDTV) and H.265 codecs will improve the experience delivered on the large and small screens alike.

Simplicity – Expectations from the consumer is at an all-time high when it comes to simplicity of watching video. The BBC iPlayer has been held up as the gold standard for delivering a rich VoD experience and Apple has lead the way with beautiful and intuitive user interface design. Both organisations have done a great job of educating everyone else on how content should be delivered and hopefully some of the horrors of the past will never be repeated again.

The opportunity for simplifying access to content is massive. Initially, film studios' and broadcasters' revenues had been relatively unscathed from online piracy compared to the traditional music industry. You will always find a small minority who won't pay for content but in a capitalist society it is actually the overwhelming majority that is happy to pay a fair price to view a TV show or film. I was involved in helping to deliver the world's first all-platform release of the feature film Road to Guantanamo written and directed by Michael Winterbottom in March 2006. Nearly ten years have passed but it still feels like the studios should be doing more to embrace the connected world.

Initiatives like UltraViolet, where a digital/mobile version is included with the DVD or Blu-ray, will certainly help to prolong the life of physical formats. However, it will come down to the simplicity of communicating the message to the consumer and you may just find that the consumer will go straight to digital to access videos in the future.

PH: There are several important things to reiterate from what Jon says. Firstly, it is key to realise that the way in which users will consume video will evolve massively over the next ten years. What we have experienced in the last few years is only the tip of the iceberg. Videos need to be ready to be played on all devices and all platforms – even those not invented and available yet. This boils down to a simple thought: you need to make sure that your video plays as well on any of the social network platforms as it plays on your website. I've had a feeling for a few years that a massive spend on making an all-singing and dancing website may not be money well spent. Instead you should be thinking about the 'content hub' idea, as well as how your website should really be only one of the ways in which you get your message across. Websites will remain paramount for anyone involved in selling products directly to consumers – that is a given. But for everyone else the imperative to have an amazing website (an imperative which ruled the roost in the early days of the internet) has been replaced by a need to ensure that your content is interesting, easily accessible and relevant to the consumer and that it is a part of your overall communication strategy.

Secondly, the barrier to entry in terms of cost is now much lower than it ever was. This is not only true in financial terms of actually producing the video – you don't need a TV budget to make successful online video as long as you have a good enough creative. But it's also the case in terms of storage, encoding and distribution.

Thirdly, quality of image. While it has been the case for some time that 'lo-fi' image quality has been accepted as the norm with some internet videos, viewer expectations are also changing, and you should strive to make your video look as sharp as possible (note that this may not necessarily apply to intentionally 'lo-fi' looking videos, which will still have a shelf life).

Q: How/why do some companies use short-form videos well, and other companies badly? What are some of the mistakes you see?

JS: When talking to companies about online video content they are sometimes disappointed by previous attempts where the completion rate and number of viewers has been low. Usually the first question I will be asked is if the video should have been shorter and my response is nearly always no. It is true that shorter videos tend to have a higher engagement but longer videos have their place.

For anyone starting out in creating or commissioning video content, I would suggest a mix of content types. Customers will want to consume video on a variety of devices and at different times of the day. Testing creative ideas and formats will allow you to analyse what works and then keep refining and evolving these formats to target your customer needs.

'Power users' who have already engaged with your brand through social platforms like YouTube will expect to be pushed regular content. Understanding what they like by analysing analytics and asking for direct feedback will help shape the type of videos you produce and result in increased views and dwell time.

The rise in mobile, tablet devices and connected TVs is already increasing dwell time and a recent Informa report forecasts that over 227m connectable TVs will be sold worldwide in 2016.

PH: The idea of content 'mix' is key. Your video shouldn't just be an instant win, but rather part of your overall strategy. And this, coupled with the above discussion of lower costs, can mean that you now have the chance to create a variety of lengths of film. Certainly a short, punchy and innovative video can grab viewers' attention – but now it's relatively affordable to create a mix of short, medium and longer-form films. Longer videos on a specific subject may well reward you with longer-term relationships with your customers as the longer they watch and are interested, the deeper your relationship with them will become. With the rapid rise in Connected TVs and services such as Netflix and Amazon Prime, users are becoming more and more used to watching long-form content over the net. We made our first longer-form documentaries in 2014 for clients who simply couldn't have considered them budget-wise in 2004: I would estimate that the costs were at least half of what they were then.

Q: Do you think it is possible to predict conversion rates for online video or is it all just smoke and mirrors?

JS: Yes it's more than possible, it's a certainty! The beauty of online is all activity can be measured and tracked back to the user.

PH We discuss click attribution and metrics elsewhere but it's essential to underline just how important it is. Even in 2016, there are plenty of companies who think a quick viral success will turn their fortunes around. This short-term mentality can often result in failure, especially if it is not part of an integrated campaign. And there are plenty of free (or cheap) tools available to you to track just how successful your video is — not just in terms of pure views, but in terms of follow-through and conversion. Once your video is released it is essential to be on top of all of this to chart its success (or failure, and then do something about it).

Q: How important is mobile in the future of online video?

The big trend will be the move from consuming online video at home to becoming more of an individual experience with viewing on personal devices and receiving recommendations based on viewing behaviour. It is not just watching video on your mobile that will be important in the future but the ability to record and share your own experiences instantly.

Smartphones have already overtaken PC shipments. The Apple iPad, launched in April 2010, kickstarted the tablet revolution, with Amazon's Kindle Fire and Google Nexus quickly following.

'Second screening', where the viewer uses both TV and mobile devices while watching simultaneously, will start to become more prevalent within the next year and Social TV services like Zeebox (now beamly) and Shazam will be integrated further into TV shows and advertising.

PH: The 'second screen' is one of the new Holy Grails of TV and social, and I've been involved in it since the early days of TV interactivity in the

1990s. But I'm not sure that anyone has really cracked it: some of the services which try to 'force' themselves into a viewer's habits may end up as off-putting. In fact, it's possible that the leaders in this area, if there are any, may emerge through a serendipitous side-effect of a pre-existing service. It's definitely a space to be watched.

What do you think are the key aspects of 'social' that companies should think about when making a short-form/online video?

YouTube is the largest social video platform but so many people forget this and just see it as a hosting platform to embed video.

Companies should invest time in building an audience of 'real engaged users', encouraging sharing of content, tweets, likes... and making sure that video is part of your wider social media strategy.

Test and learn by interacting with viewers socially, and evolve web formats by asking for direct feedback. Experiment with social media around your video content too maybe asking the audience to decide what they would like the next video to be.

Twitter has the ability to show very clearly the patterns of engagement around your video content and can be used to create a social media 'buzz' around what you are producing. Upload behind the scenes pictures and get followers to interact.

PH Many good ideas here about how to avoid the 'lonely YouTube channel'.

WHY THIS IS THE BEST HEADLINE EVER*

The act of finding the right headline for online articles and videos has evolved considerably in the last few years. The likes of Buzzfeed and Upworthy have almost turned it into a science, and there is a lot of good reading out there about how to create the perfect title in order to lure readers or viewers in.

Of course, once users become accustomed to new styles, they will adapt mentally, and what may have been fresh and 'must-see' six months ago may turn into something predictable and unclickable. This is a problem that both Upworthy and Buzzfeed are likely to face. With standard headers such as 'You'll never believe what happened next' or 'No 26 on this list is a doozie' becoming more and more familiar, readers and viewers are less likely to click through.

Over the years, with hundreds of videos released in various campaigns, we've spent a lot of time thinking what to call each one. A lot. If you are lucky you might find someone in your organisation who has the knack of writing them well. If not, it really is essential to take the time to consider what is going to have the maximum effect. A few things to think about are the length (shorter is always better), the tone (you want to try and persuade people that viewing your video will be of specific benefit to them), how well and accurately you are describing the short film (don't try and dupe people). Consider whether using the word 'you' is right for your video - using 'you' in any header can have a strong effect, but over-using it can be a danger. If you're releasing a series of videos, then you're going to have to think about how to keep your titles fresh and varied, while at the same time making sure people know it is part of a series they may either already be familiar with and liked or, if they are new to it, to ensure that they will go back and check out the other films. You'll also need to think about the secondary title, or the information paragraph: YouTube, for example, allows you to write a longer description of what is contained in the video.

It's similar to the newspaper business where editors spend a lot of time getting headlines just right. Think of it like this, and it may even be worth hiring the services of a professional copywriter to give your headlines maximum power. There are even online resources in which you can type in a headline and you receive a score based on its potential 'impact'.

Great content, and especially shareable content, will always overcome a predictable or bad headline, but the art of naming a video is extremely important.

*Or not.

HOW LONG SHOULD MY VIDEO BE?

The simple answer is that videos should be as long as they need to be, whether they be intended as corporate (for internal use, for a specified number of viewers etc) or viral. No longer, and no shorter, to get the message or the joke across. Nothing irks viewers more than a short video that is actually longer than it needs to be (apart perhaps from the pre-roll ads that come up on YouTube videos which promise 'Your video will play in 30 seconds', but that's another story).

It's become very popular to assume that attention spans have become shorter and that as a result videos should automatically become shorter. And while in general I am a fan of brevity, this shouldn't be a hard and fast rule – the correct answer is always that the video should be as long as it needs to be. If attention spans really were becoming shorter then very few people would have the patience to watch a television programme, let alone a whole film, yet conversely the average running time of a Hollywood film has actually increased over the last few years. It's about finding the right balance: how long do you need to tell whatever story you are trying to tell? And can you avoid the urge to fall in love with your video so much so that it becomes bloated, with everything including the kitchen sink being featured in it?

However, I have created some guidelines for the different types of video that may help. They aren't hard and fast rules, but they should give an idea of what works in each environment:

Virals: The standard comedy virals really can have a range of lengths, but two lengths is about the maximum cut-off I like to see, unless it's really unique or exceptional. If it's a visual gag that can be seen and understood in five seconds, then make the video five seconds. Don't force it and make it any longer than it needs to be. Vines are six seconds long, for example.

Overview video: An 'overview' video shows what your company does in an eye-catching way. They are particularly popular for start-up companies who use them to explain their concept in a short space of time. Quite often they are graphics-based and accompanied by an upbeat instrumental track. It's worth looking around at new companies to see what is in vogue: in 2010 it was an infographic style, in 2012 it was all the rage to mimic the short overview ads that Google were making. Whatever the style, the key thing to remember for anyone considering making an overview video is not to overcomplicate it. Figure out what the core value or proposition of your company is and focus on that: how will it apply to your users, how will it affect them, and why will it make them go 'Wow! I want to sign up now!'

I have seen far too many overview videos ruined because the company wants to throw every single detail in. Users don't really care about the complicated back-end procedures you may have come up with - they just want the simple message here and now. Keep it simple. Overview videos should be roughly 60-90 seconds long. Don't worry if they are shorter - you may be able to get your message across in 30 or 45 seconds. Think of mainstream, expensive, TV advertising - ads usually focus on getting the message across simply in a very short space of time. You should be trying to do the same.

Campaign videos: We've made many very successful videos for charity campaigns. If you are running an appeal and are trying to raise a seven figure sum (or more) over the course of a year or two, then you are going to need not one, but several videos. And you are going to need different versions of the same video for the various events, ceremonies, social networks, TV cutdowns, and shopping mall TV channels that suddenly offer you an opportunity.

So you need a plan.

Your main appeal video should really be a short film. It should contain all the key elements necessary to get the message across and therefore you can afford to *let it breathe*. This is especially the case if you are showing it at a large evening event/dinner where you have a captive audience. If you have a stylish, interesting film with a punchy message then you can easily afford 3-5 minutes. Any more and it *really* has to be interesting. Once you start getting over six minutes you risk alienating your audience, especially if they have spent the evening being wined and dined. If you expect them to dig deep into their pockets after a nine-minute appeal film then you may have a problem. So for a main, introductory appeal film I like the 3-5 minute timing.

But remember the plan.

If you hire a good production company to film your main campaign film, tell them to get plenty of extra footage on subjects that are associated with but not necessarily integral to your main appeal message. Try and think of all of this in advance so that once you have paid for the film crew to turn up you can maximise their time. It is also worth asking the film crew for any advice and input they have along these lines, explain your long term plan to them as they hopefully will have knowledge and experience of this kind of strategy and may think of things you didn't. If they are going to interview people then add in some extra - but related - subjects to talk about. What you are trying to do here is to get enough material from your main filming to provide you with 5 or

6 subsidiary films that you can feed out over the course of your campaign. Filming is expensive: make the most of it.

Let's imagine you are in charge of a campaign to raise £2m for improving the plight of those suffering from ingrown toenails. A typical one-year campaign might have the following films:

Main film: 3 - 5 mins
Film 2: 1 minute in which interviewee from main film (someone afflicted by the condition) talks about the effect the money would have on him.
Film 3: 1 minute in which someone from the main film talks about the fundraising they have done to help those with ingrown toenails.
Film 4: 1 minute. A day in the life of an ingrown toenail sufferer.
Final film: 2 minutes. Final push. A round-up of some of the events and progress of the campaign over the year using footage you have received from those involved, as well as a clever re-edit of the original material to get across a message like 'We're nearly there!'

What's particularly effective about this, especially given the shrinking budgets available, is that you can pre-plan so much of this in advance, and save yourself a lot of money by filming as much as possible when you make the main film. Getting a film crew out is expensive, so when you have them, maximise them.
Corporate/communications videos:

A client once said to me when we pitched them some ideas for a corporate communications idea: The problem is that the message we are getting across is so boring that nobody ever watches these videos. This can often be the case if you are trying to send out a video to 1,000 or more people in a large organisation about something to do with work restructuring, for example. Boring messages can produce boring videos. The client in question was able to measure that most viewers had watched their previous videos for only 30 seconds before turning them off.

Another issue in corporate communications videos is workforce resistance. Especially if you are introducing a new scheme that will directly impact your viewers and likely upset some of them (any new work initiative is guaranteed to irritate some of the staff).

In this situation I recommend two important strategies to my clients: honesty and humour. Don't paper over the cracks if you are introducing a potentially difficult new programme. Be upfront and honest about it and try and involve staff members from all levels. Otherwise you may come across as a purveyor of a 1984-style 'Doublespeak'. And if you want to really keep people watching, then inject some humour. Use some members of staff. We have gained a reputation for videos which spoof films or TV programmes using staff members - people love that, and the videos are far more likely to be watched all the way through.

WHO IS YOUR LEGAL EAGLE?

Throughout the book – from the interview with Eleonora Rosati and the piece on Psy/FIFA, we've discussed legal implications of publishing a video. If you are using pre-existing footage, does it need to be cleared? The same applies to music. Are you potentially libelling or defaming anyone with your video? Or are there any other legal implications which you may not have thought about but a sharp-eyed lawyer will spot?

You do have a sharp-eyed lawyer, right?

If you are producing a lot of video content on behalf of a company or organisation, then it's fairly important that you get everything checked by legal before it is published. This in itself can be problematic, especially with companies who haven't latched onto the fact that there is going to be an implied cost of the lawyer's time to check everything. Another reason it can cause an issue is if the lawyer is not on the same page: despite its being 2016, there are plenty of lawyers who trained in the pre-internet age and who are still mentally working with 1980s and 1990s mindsets. They may not quite get the subtleties of what you are trying to do, or even understand the platforms you are using to distribute your videos on.

In an ideal world – and it is possible if you work for a forward-thinking company that is prepared to commit resources to the legal side of things – your lawyer will be involved (albeit with a light touch) at the key stages of the process. These are, broadly speaking, the initial idea period when they can give an advised likely 'yes' or 'no' as to whether a video may get your company in trouble or not. Then, assuming a 'yes' has been given, there is the script stage, when a lawyer can really look at the detail of what you are planning to do and point out any potential dangers. Lastly, the lawyer will need to look at the final product before it is released (final videos and interpretations will always have slight differences from what may have come across in the script).

Furthermore, in order for this all to happen, you need to have a savvy, with-it lawyer (as described above), and one who is prepared, or has the time, to react quickly to any of your questions. One who is able to review your proposals and work in good time. And all of this will have to be okayed by your chain-of-command, for as we said at the outset of this section, there is very much a cost associated with all of this. Problematic lawyers, or complex approval processes (we've got a good example of this later with the Twitter approval process employed by Mitt Romney's 2012 Presidential campaign), can delay publication of your video, and if you are working on a timed or rapid-reaction response video, then this can almost render your video out-of-date by the time it is released.

GAMIFICATION

The notion of turning everything into a 'game' has been a hot online potato in the last few years, especially since Foursquare came to prominence around 2010. Human resource departments have even tried to figure out how to turn workplaces into 'gaming' areas, with the notion that encouraging workers to strategise and win points in their day-to-day routine would increase performance. It is, however, a tricky area: when was the last time anyone you knew checked in to become the virtual mayor of anywhere?

It all boils down to the fact that consumers are often far more savvy than companies – especially in the digital sphere – and it's this 'one step ahead' phenomenon that can catch companies out. This is why turning a video release into a 'game' can have negative consequences. If you are rewarding people for retweeting your video, or sharing it as widely as possible, then you may end up simply annoying them – or more likely their friends. People want to feel like they have discovered a video on their own, whether it be from a trusted source or member of their peer group. Sharing it confers a degree of pride upon them, but 'false' sharing (such as retweeting just to gain points for a certain scheme) can soon lead to a steep drop-off in real interaction.

ARE THE FIRST FIVE SECONDS OF YOUR VIDEO STRONG ENOUGH?

Viewers are extremely active (rather than passive) when it comes to online videos. The keyboard or mobile screen acts as a kind of TV remote control for them. When people are flicking through the TV with their remote, it usually takes only a few seconds to figure out what they are watching and if they are going to stick on that channel. The same principle applies with online video: especially when people are casually surfing. They know that there are thousands of other videos out there that they could be looking at – so why this one, and why now?

This is why the idea that the first five seconds of a video must be attention-grabbing has become increasingly popular. Grab them straight away, the theory goes, and you'll keep them watching. There is an element of truth in this – and the opening of any video, short or even feature should certainly try to engage the viewer's attention. And it's especially relevant to videos on Facebook where visual trumps audio at the start of a video: Facebook videos are typically presented with the volume turned down. But if the first five seconds are followed by poorly-conceived content, viewers will be equally likely to click away. So while you should give the first five seconds of your video a good deal of thought, don't do so at the expense of the rest of it.

CASE STUDY: HOW OUR DRAGONS' DEN HELPED LOCAL GOVERNMENT COMMUNICATE

East Sussex County Council had a problem. Nobody was watching their in-house communications videos. They knew this because they were tracking engagement. Very few of their messages from the top managers were watched all the way through by their thousands of staff.

The council had been forward-thinking enough to figure out that video was a great way of explaining new initiatives and policies. But the videos that they made lacked engagement and shareability. They usually consisted of talking heads dictating a new programme. They didn't make any of the staff want to discuss the issues over the water cooler.

So the council asked us to help. They wanted to launch a new directive, and this time they wanted to make sure that the video hit the sweet spot. We worked with them and developed the idea of making their own short version of 'Dragons' Den' (the business programme known as 'Shark Tank' in the US). We recruited a panel of five 'Dragons' from departments and levels across the council – members of staff who would be directly affected by the directive. They would question the manager responsible for the new project in a spoof of the TV show. It was good-natured, but we prompted the staff to pull no punches and really drill down with their questions.

The shoot day was great fun: we created a spoofy menacing opening titles sequence using the council buildings, and recreated our own version of the theme tune.

Prior to its release the council built up interest by running a countdown to the release date, as well as posting pictures of the shoot on their intranet. Everyone knew someone involved in the day. They hosted internal screenings of the short on the day of release.

The result: far greater interaction and interest in the video. The message got across. Staff members did discuss it. And they watched it all the way through.

Using members of staff can be a great way of promoting engagement and getting the message across: especially if you come at it from a new angle.

THE CEO SPEAKS

In the Autumn of 2013, the CEO of one of the world's leading pasta-makers, Barilla, got his company into trouble – big trouble. During an interview meant to extol the quality of his market-leading pasta, the CEO made comments that were perceived as being homophobic. He would never, he admitted, use a homosexual couple in one of his ad campaigns.

The resulting furore, both justified and completely expected, was far and wide: around the world current and potential Barilla buyers were aghast. Some even proposed a boycott. The company did its best to mollify the complaints, but it soon became clear they were fighting a losing battle: despite video apologies by the CEO and a firefighting campaign by its many marketing and PR agencies, it's likely that Barilla's reputation will have undoubtedly been tarnished for a sizeable amount of its customer base. And, as tasty and high quality as it is, there are probably five to ten other pastas out there of equal deliciousness.

This is why you need to think very carefully before you make the CEO of your company the star of your video.

Quite often someone at the top of the company decides to star in their own video. This can range from a straightforward piece to camera, perhaps talking about the origin or purpose or aim of the company, to doing something 'wacky' to gain attention. 'Wackiness' can work, but usually only if the CEO or equivalent is inherently charismatic and game. Never force a stiff or taciturn CEO into doing something on camera they may live to regret or may harm your company's image. Victor Kiam pioneered this kind of thing when he declared 'I liked the shaver so much, I bought the company'. But he was able to meld a certain level of wackiness while at the same time putting across the fact that he had business acumen. George Foreman did the same with his range of grills.

Whatever you decide, make sure your CEO is 'telegenic' enough to be on camera. Even after media training I have seen far too many videos of extraordinarily dull top-level people who decide it is their right to lead the video. It's nearly always a mistake. And if they are a loose cannon, and likely to blurt out something inappropriate like the Barilla executive, then you need to block his or her appearance completely.

If you look at the likes of Michael O'Leary and Richard Branson, as well as the former Yahoo! CEO Carole Bartz and the new incumbent Marissa Meyer, you can see examples of just how the CEO's personality needs to be used very carefully when it comes to video and TV appearances. O'Leary, the charismatic CEO of Ryanair, has made a career out of putting people's backs up: here is a CEO who is not afraid to criticise even his own customers. Yet he is savvy enough to realise his shortcomings, as he announced in a 2013 conference when referring to the seemingly offhand manner in which his company treats its passengers. O'Leary just about manages to contain his outspoken character (he also manages to run one of the world's most popular and profitable airlines, whatever his detractors say).

Richard Branson is the perfect example of a CEO who has enough recognition, chutzpah and charisma to be a great visual leader for his array of companies: from the early days of his Virgin Atlantic airline, Branson was pulling stunts that no other CEO would dare: from his various cross-dressing exploits to having some of the world's biggest celebrities work with him (one of his latest campaigns has Usain Bolt dressed up as Branson), Branson is a one-man advertising campaign.

The internet giant Yahoo! went through some tricky times under the leadership of Carole Bartz from 2009 - 2011. Bartz was possibly as forthright as Michael O'Leary at Ryanair, but she failed to charm the press, and her outspoken outbursts – she wasn't afraid to unleash four-letter words when it suited her - may eventually have helped her demise in 2011. After a long search and one or two false steps, a long-term successor was finally chosen in Marissa Mayer. Mayer, an internet thoroughbred who had made her name at Google, showed again just how CEOs need to be very careful: in an early video interview, she raised some hackles with some arguably easy-to-misinterpret comments about childcare (while banning working from home and extolling the need to find a good work-life balance, Mayer had a nursery constructed in her office for her new child). But in 2013, when delivering the company's annual earning reports, Mayer decided to do things differently: instead of providing the usual boring teleconference on dry statistics, Mayer co-anchored a news bulletin which was broadcast to all the waiting journalists, providing all of the facts and figures. Sure, it was a little bit stilted and clumsy in places, but it also had plenty of appeal: so much so that it was an impressive piece of CEO-generated content. Mayer certainly seems to be on the right track – in the summer of 2013, it was announced that Yahoo! had overtaken Google in terms of web traffic in the United States, something that would have been probably regarded as inconceivable during the Bartz era.

So – in summary – we need to reiterate the earlier sentence: think VERY carefully before you make the CEO of your company the star of your video.

EL DORITOS

In 2009, before our company really even existed, we entered another competition. The makers of the crisp brand 'Doritos' had a massive video competition, where users could make and upload their own home-made 'ads'. The winner would receive cash, and their ad would be shown on TV.

These competitions can be a very useful tool for start-up video providers. It helps them to get their head around working to a brief and if there are a lot of entries, it's a good way of gauging just how good your creative and execution is compared to others. And if you win, or do something really special, it can often act as a springboard to bigger things.

My Handface partner Lisa made a very funny video in which she developed a whole band of roving Mariachi players, who toured around England bringing joy – and Doritos – to anyone they met. It was well-shot, well-acted, funny, but it didn't win.

Fast-forward to 18 months later when we started receiving text messages and emails from friends about the *actual* brand new Doritos ad that was airing on British TV. Lo and behold it featured a whole band of roving Mariachi players, who toured England and brought joy – and Doritos – to anyone they met. The similarities to our ad were, to put it simply, quite spectacular. And it wasn't just friends and family members who noticed the difference: shortly after we were contacted by the satirical magazine Private Eye who had also noticed the similarities.

Private Eye even went so far as to contact the advertising agency who made the ad, who strenuously denied that anything underhand had taken place, and that any resemblance between the two ads was merely coincidental. This is fair enough, and I should reiterate for legal reasons that in no way am I accusing anyone of any theft of intellectual property. It's not a stretch of the imagination for more than one person to have an idea that links Doritos to roving Mariachi players.

But the lesson here isn't about me moaning that an idea we had may or may not have been taken and worked on by somebody else. It's that this kind of thing happens all the time: 'exclusivity' of ideas is often a grey area. It's a very hot potato in the comedy world, with stand-ups deeply frowning on anyone who may purportedly have pinched a gag, and Tweeters blowing a gasket if they think their original work has been stolen. But in the world of online video, especially parody or amusing videos, it's often inevitable that more than one person will have a similar idea at the same time about the same subject. So, unless it's blatant daylight robbery, accept it and move on.

INTERVIEW: AMANDA WILKIE

Amanda Wilkie is a social media creative for the company That Lot. She also writes comedy videos and visual jokes for Huffington Post UK's comedy department. Her comedy work has been featured in newspapers, on the internet and on television on many occasions. Amanda operates at the coalface of video discovery: often finding clips which have just been released and are yet to go viral. Any company really interested in finding viral videos should have an Amanda. On Twitter she is @Pandamoanimum.

Q: How would you describe what you do in terms of finding little-seen comedy videos?

AW: I have certain websites that I visit that source funny videos, amongst them are sites where people post their own videos so this means I will often see these when they've been barely viewed as they're still very new. I'm not always spot on but I do seem to have quite an instinct for knowing what will possibly go viral or become an 'internet sensation'. I suppose my general attitude is that if I find it amusing then I assume other people will too.

PH: Already we can see the sheer range of videos that are out there and how difficult it can be to get your video seen.

Q: What are the kinds of subjects that make videos go viral, in your opinion (eg Is comedy king?)

AW: People hurting themselves/being made to look foolish in some way and animals/children doing funny/silly things are what instantly spring to mind in answer to that.

PH: *These are, of course, just some of the things that can make a video go viral, and explains the success of TV shows such as You've Been Framed. Of course if we take this to an extreme, vindictive videos are probably not the best way to go, but accidentally amusing videos can often become huge successes. One issue companies may have is trying to 'recreate' in some shape or form these accidental videos. Viewers are now savvy enough to spot when they are being fed something fake (one of the most common questions about a supposedly amazing piece of video that relies on an extraordinary juxtaposition of events, which is simultaneously filmed at the same time, is 'Is it a fake'?) But there is even a growing trend of appreciating fake videos – if the subject matter is original and if the video is well made. However, I generally advise companies not to attempt to create their own fake videos – shorts such as Charlie Bit My Finger are once in a lifetime occurrences, and companies can waste a lot of time and money making something that can often backfire on them.*

Q: How important are Twitter and Facebook in making something popular? Are there any other platforms which are important - and does email still have a role to play?

AW: Twitter is VERY important. If you read a news report after a video has gone viral then the majority of the time it will note Twitter has being the reason it spread so rapidly. Facebook will occasionally throw out something that becomes a hit, but it's normally something Facebook-related: a certain status or a Facebook user's own video that they posted there but not on Twitter. It's a bit of a standing joke on Twitter that Facebook is always a few days behind on anything funny or topical. In regard to videos, I don't think there are any other platforms that are as important as Twitter for getting hits on YouTube or the like. I personally don't think email really has a role to play at all. I tweet, RT or Facebook status update funny things and I think most do the same. It wouldn't even occur to me to email friends the link to a funny video I'd just seen. Without meaning to sound unkind or ageist, emailing a funny thing, be it a video, a joke etc is the type of thing I'd expect my mum or dad to do...the older generation. The ones who have just discovered how to poke people on Facebook and still think Twitter is a place where all people do is tweet about their lunch. If, on the rare occasion, I do get sent a video by email I can pretty much guarantee it will be something I've seen days if not weeks before.

PH I think this is a hugely important answer for several reasons, and we will discuss the differences in reactions to video on Facebook and Twitter in greater depth later. The main thing to reiterate however, is the timelag between the two platforms. Twitter is much more 'of the moment', and certainly watching a video spreading across Twitter shows how instant and powerful it is. Facebook, for reasons we will go into later, does tend to lag behind. Quite often I also see videos, which have already passed their sell-by date on Twitter, appearing on Facebook a few days later. This isn't necessarily always a negative though: it can show that the video has really spread into the wider consciousness. But in terms of instant impact and measuring the success of a video in the short-term then Twitter is usually a much more reliable guide.

Amanda's comment about email also shows the fluid and changing nature in which we use the internet. Until Facebook really took off, it was still more common to email viral gags, but as she points out, emailing them now is very much the preserve of the older generation who may finally be turning to the internet and email. But this is a generation which will start to die out: the children of the internet (who are the customers of tomorrow) would rarely think of sharing a video via email these days, and that is not something that is going to come back into fashion. However, that is not to say that email itself is dying out: it seems to be undergoing something of a marketing resurgence, which I will discuss elsewhere.

But there is also another – increasingly important – way of sharing, and that is through private groups on services such as WhatsApp. Sometimes referred to as 'grey social', it's not public and therefore not publicly measurable. For various reasons not everyone wants to share on a public social network all of the time: they might be afraid of the impression it will give, any potential backlash, or they might just be more comfortable sharing it with a trusted group. More on this below.

Q: How important is a celebrity 'endorsement' in helping a video grow in terms of views?

AW: Hugely important. Massively so. You could tweet the funniest video ever but if you've only got 10 followers then there's very little chance it'll get any sort of views. It really is all about numbers. The more followers, the more chance of it getting out there. And the celebrities are the ones with the big numbers. Plus, their fans like to please them and so I sometimes think people will RT things because 'If Mr A. Celeb thinks it's worthy of tweeting/RT-ing then it must be REALLY funny'. Though I think it can also be 'luck'. Someone can tweet something and it just needs to get RT'd by the 'right' person and it can then have a massive ripple effect. For example, one Sunday morning, I tweeted a funny thing I'd found, someone RT-d it who wasn't famous but who was being followed by someone slightly higher up the Twitter chain. It was then RT'd by someone following that person who was semi-famous. They were being followed by someone more famous who RT'd it etc etc until it was just being RT'd by thousands. If I'd have tweeted it 10 minutes earlier or later then it might have come to nothing and I'd have been left sitting muttering 'Well I thought it was funny anyway'.

PH While the power of the celebrity retweet certainly still carries weight (and I explained my own story of this when we looked at the importance of the MP Tom Watson retweeting our Hackgate video), there is a 'however' to this answer. Simply put, celebrities are themselves increasingly savvy to the phenomenon. Imagine you are Stephen Fry (during one of the times he is on Twitter with his millions of followers), and then imagine the amount of unsolicited Tweets you would receive every day. Finding the time alone to look at all of them is one thing, and then making the decision to retweet them is another, given the power that you would have. This is why certain celebrities have left Twitter, or take occasional Twitter breaks – the sheer volume of information they receive would be mindboggling to the average Twitter user, let alone the amount of contrary opinions (ok let's call it trolling) that they have to deal with.

So if you are a company relying on a celebrity retweet, think carefully. Are you going to spend a lot of time and effort based on the notion that a celebrity will retweet it? Studies have even been made about the actual financial value of a celebrity retweet which, in some instances, can run into the thousands of dollars. Most celebrities who have some experience of Twitter will realise this and may be unwilling to be a pawn in your game.

But, as Amanda points out, there can be a huge upside in terms of numbers of views. We have made videos that include celebrities (and I'll explain later how Fry himself featured in our Los 33 spoof and yes, he retweeted it to great effect). If the celebrity is in the video and is well represented, then there is more of a chance that he or she will retweet. If the subject matter is an area of special interest to a celebrity then they may also be interested in sharing it. But if it's a desperate call to get a celebrity to retweet a promotional video, then your chances may be a lot slimmer. (Note to charities: I do wonder about the actual value of having a celebrity retweet your appeal message. There may be an upside in creating some awareness, but it would be interesting to see the follow-up stats on how many people click through to the appeal and then actually donate).

Of course if you have enough of a budget to have a celebrity as part of your marketing campaign then you should certainly try and milk this for as much as it is worth. Yet even this needs to be thought through carefully – readers will definitely be put off by overt pleas on behalf of the celebrity. It can be incredibly successful if done well however, and the Columbian actress Sofia Vergara's Twitter account is a very good example. Vergara, reportedly the highest-paid actress on US TV thanks to her starring role in 'Modern Family', is an accomplished Tweeter (with just under 9 million followers at the time of writing). Her Twitter account is an entertaining mix of photos and information about her glamorous life – from behind the scenes shots of rehearsals for her sitcom, as well as images from some of the many promotional campaigns she undertakes. Yet it is all very naturally communicated, and gives the impression that Vergara herself is in charge of her own account. The value to the brands that pay her to promote their goods is therefore enormously enhanced in the social media sphere thanks to the simple and fun way that their ambassador comes across – certainly not forced and certainly not desperate.

One final thing to bear in mind on celebrities is that it is essential to both choose the right one to use in your campaign, and to have a plan in place just in case it backfires. If a celebrity gets caught up in a scandal, for example, would your company's name be tainted by association?

Q: Are there 'trends' in video virals? In term of subject matter/style etc?

AW: Yes. I think Gangnam Style then Harlem Shake were two pretty extreme examples of this. If a video goes viral, then you can pretty much always expect parodies etc to follow immediately after. Or if there's a funny animal video, for example 'Goats that shout like humans', then you can normally expect similar style videos to start doing the rounds.

PH You could mention any of the 'Frozen' tributes that emerged in 2014, or the hundreds of versions of 'Happy' by Pharrell Williams. Once someone had made a 'goat that sang like Taylor Swift' video early in 2013, for example, we were one of the many people who made their own compilation of 'goat-singing' videos.

Q: 'It's impossible to actually create a really good viral – most of them are happy accidents'. What's your view on this?

AW: I think this is pretty much an accurate statement. There's obviously a percentage that are set up and created that go huge, but I think the majority of those that go really massive are the ones where there is an element of shock/surprise etc. The moments that if they hadn't been caught on camera then, would probably never occur again.

FACEBOOK VS TWITTER

Let's look in a little more depth at the differences between Facebook and Twitter, especially vis-à-vis how social videos work on both platforms. In terms of how videos are shared from person to person, they are currently still the dominant means of communication (leaving email lagging some distance behind), so they deserve closer inspection as there are important differences between the two.

Twitter:

With over 200 million users sending an average of over 500 million tweets a day (a figure that was growing up to the start of 2015), Twitter is an essential medium for sharing viral video. There are plenty of easy-to-access metrics available as well to show you how your video is performing: not just the number of people who may have personally retweeted or favourited a video of yours (although I've personally never really seen the point of favouriting a tweet), but the *potential audience* (ie all the followers of someone who has posted the retweet), which can often be huge and give you an excellent ROI in terms of visibility, expanding your audience and promoting your message.

If you want to know the reaction to current news or sports events, then Twitter is the place to be. Therefore it follows that in terms of the speed at which a video is currently shared, there is no doubt that Twitter is the king. Or queen. It has a slightly less personal nature to it than Facebook – Twitter users are more likely to have a mix of people and organisations they follow, than the pure friends feed on Facebook. So typically a Twitter user will follow friends, celebrities, organisations they are interested in or use, and any information outlets about specific hobbies or interests they have. 'Unfollowing' someone on Twitter is much less of a big deal than 'Unfriending' someone on Facebook.

Because it is essentially much more of a 'live' medium, and because it restricts posts to a succinct 140 characters or fewer, the sheer volume of information travelling through it is massive. And so are the interaction and sharing capabilities. Because of this, it is the first destination for viral videos to initially spread from. Watching a new video take off on Twitter, with large numbers of retweets per second or minute, is actually quite an exhilarating experience (if that's your bag). And if someone with a large number of followers retweets your video, then the number of views can increase wildly, as the video is passed along the chain to other people with large numbers of followers.

What Twitter shares with Facebook, however, is the possibility of a backlash. Social network users, especially those who use Twitter, are often far more savvy than the companies that are trying to engage them. They can sniff out any exploitative campaigns and 'fails' and as a result the negative feedback can be dramatic.

And it's important to realise that Twitter is also changing. Its position as the golden child of the social media world is undergoing something of a change – due to a number of reasons. It may have reached saturation point in terms of active users (while it has an estimated 10 million signed up users in the UK, the active userbase must be dramatically lower).
The average Twitter user has somewhat solidified into a certain type of person. It's a stereotype to say it but it has now arguably become the tool of the 'elite'. This idea was first mooted to me at a Guardian Open Day lecture in 2012 when my first reaction was to disbelieve it. 'How could something that was so transparent and

open be used in an elitist way?', I thought. But as time has progressed, Twitter has arguably edged towards elitism. It's a shouty place where an awful lot of people are clamouring to be heard.

This has subsequently had the effect of shifting some users back to Facebook (where the pace is much more sedate) and it will probably mean that the overall active userbase will plateau over the next few years (there's even an argument to say the number might reduce). So, while Twitter is currently *the* place for a video to really start its viral path, it's important to remember just who exactly is using it – success on Twitter may not be the be-all and end-all it once was. Like any other social network, Twitter may not be for everyone.

In the final quarter of 2014, Twitter released what has been described as a 'dockable' video function – something that YouTube has had for a while – which allows users to both watch Twitter videos in their feed as well as tapping the video to allow it to play at the bottom of the screen while continuing to read their Twitter feed. It's a positive step in terms of video, as it will encourage more people to watch and, ideally, share.

Around the same time, Twitter also released an analytics dashboard which allows advertisers and verified users to see all sorts of relevant and fascinating information: engagement levels via the number of link clicks, retweets, favourites and so on. This will help in the key areas of figuring out what exactly is working best for you in terms of *when* your content is working and *what type* of content is working for you.

One other key area in which Twitter has outperformed its social rivals is the perception the media has of it. Twitter is, in short, the media's darling. This is undoubtedly because of user bias – reporters love Twitter, and use it far more than the average person, so they tend to look at it as both an information feed and as a representation of the zeitgeist. It's now common to see a report on a 'social' story include several quotes from random Twitter users. What this means is that Twitter is a more likely way of getting your viral video into the mainstream press.

Facebook:

The grand old duke (or dame) of social networks, Facebook is also undergoing huge transformations in how people are using it, and more pointedly who is using it. One issue that has been much discussed in the last year or two is that the influx of older people (parents, aunts and grandmothers) has led to an exodus of its traditional core userbase of younger people. But there is also an indication that a lot of people who have dallied with Twitter and have found it too 'noisy' are happy to come back to Facebook for its rather more laidback appeal.

How users interact with companies on Facebook is also a different matter. Whereas on Twitter they are more likely to tolerate some companies that they find useful, the fact that companies have invaded Facebook has become a source of antagonism for many Facebook users, who really want to use it as a relaxed medium to interact with their friends (and, increasingly, family). There are plenty of articles about how companies need to behave on Facebook, and the actual real-world value of being 'liked' by someone on there. Facebook is certainly trying to grab the company dollar but increasing its options vis-à-vis video: companies can now buy sponsored videos in the Facebook news feed, and it is also showing its Facebook view count – a clear attempt to take on YouTube in the video stakes.

When it comes to video, it's certainly true that Facebook lags behind Twitter in terms of speed. Very often I see videos being shared on Facebook that were already popular on Twitter days, or even weeks, before. And while some hardcore Twitter followers may mock Facebook for this reason, having a video go viral on Facebook does at least indicate that the video has gone *really* viral. So if your video has a second wave of success on Facebook, days after its first success on Twitter, you should look at this as the icing on the cake. It's indicative that a video has really embedded itself into the zeitgeist. And there are plenty of articles which suggest that Facebook may, eventually, overtake YouTube as the web's leading place to watch videos (this argument is slightly complicated by the fact that most people still post video to Facebook *from* YouTube. Until it becomes commonplace for Facebook to become the de facto hosting site for videos, YouTube will retain its numerical advantage).

One huge thing that has happened to Facebook in the last 12 months is the proliferation of native video on the site. Instead of just having video embeds from YouTube, the native Facebook video player will play videos automatically as users scroll down their feed. It's going to become an increasingly important factor in the way videos are viewed and shared.

And bear in mind that the 'share' process on Facebook and Twitter is also different because people are sharing with very different groups. On Twitter it's likely to be much more impersonal – something of a split between some friends, some celebs, some Tweeters with shared interests and some random followers, while on Facebook it's nearly all friends and family.

And as for email: it's not dead, and it won't go away, although its limitations are becoming increasingly apparent, which is why a number of solutions or alternatives to it have sprung up - but it is now, generally speaking, a very old-school way of sharing videos.

Needless to say, while Facebook and Twitter are the two biggest social networks and success on either can lead to thousands of views, you should always remember that they are vast, noisy and crowded places. There are plenty of other networks and sites out there that may be of more benefit to you, as they may be places where you can get your content to stand out. Reddit, StumbleUpon, Medium are just three examples of other sites or networks where you could target a campaign that may get you the traction you need. This is especially the case with a forum or site that is focussed on your area of interest: you could regard this as potentially a potentially primed audience which is ready to engage with you…just as long as you have the right content for them. Another growing means of sharing information and videos on a more personal scale is WhatsApp. In 2016, it has become more common to see 'share via Whatsapp' buttons embedded on websites and the statistics of sharing content on WhatsApp have significantly increased. This small-scale social sharing, in which people have different but easily accessible groups to talk to, is beginning to creep into areas previously associated with email. And the figures bear testament to it: some sports viral sites are now claiming that their share rate via WhatsApp is higher than via Twitter or Facebook. This is because small groups of sports fans love to share information that they think will be of interest only to them.

IS THE NUMBER FIVE THE FUTURE OF SOCIAL MEDIA?

I've currently got five different groups on WhatsApp who I chat with on a regular/semi-regular basis. There's a little bit of crossover in terms of the people on there (a few people are in two or three groups), but essentially each group fulfils a different purpose. A couple are interest-based (in my case sports and pop culture), a couple are friends-based and one is family-based. The average number of people in each group is also five. One has three and one has seven but the rest have five.

I'm sharing stuff in those groups: links, photos I've taken that I just want that specific group to see, and videos. But where is the fact that I am sharing video on there being acknowledged or registered? And how is anyone measuring the reactions to them – these are private groups with private comments so any 'sentiment-based' measurement tool is just not going to register it.

The prevalence of this so-called 'grey' or 'dark' social media is going to increase, and companies and analytics tools are going to be able to do very little in terms of measuring it and reacting to it. With their standard operating procedures being as slow as they are, it's going to take them ages to even understand what it is and catch up. What it means is that a lot of the information we think is accurate about who is watching our videos and what they are saying about them may not be that accurate at all. It's worth bearing in mind when considering how to measure reactions to your content.

SHOULD YOUR VIDEO BE BORING? OR SHOULD IT BE MADE FOR SHARING?

Some key details tend to get forgotten in companies' sometimes urgent need to create a viral video. These include overvaluing the percentage share rate, how exactly people are discovering the video, and the recall percentage that the video creates.

Let's imagine Company A makes a video and tracks that 5% of all viewers share it. Company B makes its own video and 10% of all viewers do likewise. Company B is the winner, right?

Not necessarily, and especially not if we take absolute numbers into consideration. Let's say the overall number of views for Company A's video is 100 million, and Company B's is 40 million. With the share rates we have applied, the total number of people that have *shared* Video A is 5 million, while the total number of people sharing Video B is 4 million. A million more people sharing a video is significant enough to drive more traffic and interest to the company's core product.

But how are the other 95 or 90% of people coming to the video? Is it through paid promotion? If so, then how can this be classed as something that is really viral? It's essential to track *how* people are coming to the video in order to get a deeper understanding of what the real reaction is.

Finally, it's possible to make the world's wackiest and most-shared video, but if nobody can remember what it is for, then it might have been a futile achievement. That's not to say that boring factual videos always win out, but there is a sweet spot of videos that have a high number of overall viewers, a high percentage share rate, and a high recall factor. That's the dream target.

YOUTUBE COMMENTS

If you've never seen the English comedian Adam Buxton presenting his live show 'Bug', then I can highly recommend it. In a hilarious hour, Buxton looks at videos on YouTube, cherry-picks the stupidest and best comments underneath and highlights the often ridiculous things that are posted.

It's fair to say that Buxton picks on easy targets, but his show does highlight how commonplace it is now for people to comment on the video-sharing network. These comments provide companies with another means of testing the success (or not) of their videos. Not only can you see the number of views (and thanks to the excellent analytic tools on YouTube, the location and age range of people who are viewing your video) but right underneath the video you have a whole range of comments – directly talking about your work/service/idea/offerings. You also get a handy little snapshot of what percentage of viewers give your video a thumbs-up or a thumbs-down.

This is an incredibly useful way for you to assess how your video has been received, and it also raises the question of how you respond. Certainly with some of the positive feedback there is an opportunity for you to boost the morale of your team. But what do you do about negative feedback? This is akin to negative comments on your company's Facebook page, and just as it does on Facebook, your response requires careful thought. After all, this is now a public forum – not just a private letter of complaint that you have to deal with.

Many companies have felt the full force of social network shaming when they have failed to deal with Facebook comments in an appropriate way, and the same mentality should apply to

YouTube comments. You have three main choices with all comments on YouTube: to do nothing visibly, leave them as is and take note of them for internal consumption. Or you could engage the user (something which has become more prevalent since it is now a common thing to do on Twitter). This has the advantage of showing you as someone who takes customer issues and complaints seriously, but it must be underlined that you have to really think about how to reply – what tone you should take, and why exactly you are replying. The third approach is to delete the negative comments: as the owner of the YouTube channel you have the power to do this. But unless the comments are inflammatory or really likely to cause deep offence, this is an ill-advised approach that can come back to haunt you, as it runs the risk of portraying you as a tyrant who cannot have anything negative said about them (and if you delete someone's negative comments, you are only likely to increase their antipathy towards you).

It's worth bearing in mind, though, that at the end of 2013, YouTube altered its comments policy so that only people with a YouTube or Google Plus account could actually comment. This caused something of an outrage online, with petitions being created to protest against it. What it means for the comments is that not just anybody can make a comment and hide behind a swiftly created nom-de-plume. So it slightly skews the comments to be from more internet-savvy users, or at least people who have gone to the next level of interaction with YouTube or Google.

INTEGRATE YOUR VIDEOS INTO YOUR WORKPLACE

It's astonishing the number of large companies that still fail to integrate their social marketing across all of the departments in their company. According to the 2013 Invesp report I referred to earlier, 'less than 20% of US companies have integrated social media with their customer service, sales or product development processes'.

This can have dramatic effects on efficiency and company morale. It should, for example, be essential that all videos are shown to the workforce before they go public. Not only does this encourage your workforce to feel involved, proud and excited but it also prepares them to act as advocates when the video is released. If it's a great video that needs a push, then having hundreds or even thousands of your workforce who are willing to spread the message across their own social network usage is an invaluable resource.

On the other hand, if the workforce knows nothing about the video because it is seen as the 'preserve' of the marketing department, then you will be continuing to operate in a late 20th century fashion. Staff may be demoralised by not being involved, confused by the final product (especially if it has humour or is abstract) and therefore much less willing to share it across their personal networks.

If you are going to buy into the social world, then you really need integration. Your team is now no longer just your advertising or marketing department: nearly every member of staff is likely to have a Facebook or Twitter account, and if they are proud of the latest video and feel part of it, then you should be able to maximise the opportunity given by these free advocates.

SOCIAL NETWORKS DON'T OPERATE 9 TO 5 HOURS: NEITHER SHOULD YOU

It's still fairly commonplace (in 2016) for companies who have decided to run social media accounts to do so on a 9 to 5 basis. Off the top of my head I can think of one national transport company and one national delivery company in the UK who operate 9 to 5 (or 6) social media policies. Which means that while they are engaged and responsive during working hours, once the evening or weekends come, they are gone.

But social networks don't operate like this.

They are time-agnostics places, where users will check Twitter in the bathroom first thing in the morning and last thing at night. And once one timezone goes to bed, another one wakes up.

If you launch a video during working hours and it has a sudden burst of popularity at 10pm, or if it causes some sort of controversy which might negatively impact your company, how are you going to react? And who is going to react on your behalf?

Companies need to really take this on board when launching a video campaign. More enlightened organisations are beginning to realise this: the concept of flexible working hours is becoming more and more prevalent. Of course, the cost has to be well-measured: you don't need or want to pay someone to sit around for hours on the off-chance that something is going to happen that requires a response. But if you think of it as having employees that are 'on-call', and are able to consider exchanging any actual out-of-hours work for time off in lieu, then you may have your social bases covered.

This is often reaffirming what employees are doing: it's actually already fairly commonplace for employees who are looking after social media and video campaigns to keep an eye on things from home in the evenings and at the weekend. Forward-thinking companies who realise this will benefit from having rapid response measures in place coupled with increased employee satisfaction.

Another issue companies need to think about in this respect is the blurred line between an employee's personal social network life and their work role online. Some employees may find it uncomfortable to have to constantly blend in tweets and Facebook statuses from a work account into their personal accounts. Companies need to develop guidelines on this: a good rule of thumb is that employees should be given the equivalent of a political 'free vote' as to whether or not to push a work message into their online social world.

WHO HAS THE PASSWORDS TO YOUR ACCOUNT?

Right now, do you know how many different social network accounts you have representing you? Either as a creator or as a company? And do you have just one YouTube account? Or several? And who knows the passwords to all of accounts?

It's a point increasingly worth considering, especially for companies. What if a disgruntled employee has your passwords and decides to publish the wrong kind of material. It could be something defamatory, inappropriate, or even your company's state secrets.

Password security needs to be taken seriously. American Airlines found out the hard way in the summer of 2014 when somebody had access to their Twitter account and posted some pornographic images. The tweets were widely circulated and it caused a PR headache for the company, as well as the financial cost of cleaning up the situation.

So – who knows your passwords and when are you next going to change them?

IS YOUR VIDEO FEEDBACK GOVERNED BY FEAR?

A key reason that videos can fail to create any traction is fear. Not necessarily the fear of failure, but the fear of pushing the boundaries a little. And to be frank this is a very common occurrence in medium to large enterprises when middle managers may have a complex chain of command above them and their input into the video may be governed by not upsetting the bosses. Meanwhile these bosses themselves are likely to be from a pre-internet background, and while they have got the basics of the internet world and social media, they haven't quite grasped what it means to really connect with their audiences or customers through the media now available to them.

This can lead to a vicious circle where middle managers may be afraid of upsetting their bosses who are themselves sometimes ignorant of trends and online potential. As a result, this can have a damaging impact on the video in question: far too often I hear from clients that they think it is in the best interest to create a video that errs on the safe side. It may be bang on-message, but it may have little of the creative impact that would really make it stand out and be talked about. You only need to look at the standout TV commercials to see how radical leaps of faith were needed to develop memorable campaigns starring animated creatures or talking dogs. This doesn't only apply to companies who have a TV budget: the smaller budgets available for online promotion can also yield great results, if a little imagination is applied and companies are willing to take a leap of faith. If you want to engage, then make the product engaging. If you want to play it safe, then you may well end up reaping little reward. Don't let your video be strangled by fear.

While we are on the subject of feedback, while it is good to take on board as many opinions as possible, it's also essential to correctly weigh up these opinions. If Jo in accounts is the only person who thinks that the font should be blue, as opposed to red, then you need to really consider how important Jo's opinion is compared to the group's. *Everyone* loves to have an opinion on videos, but effective feedback needs to weigh these opinions, and ideally blend them as a whole to provide one coherent voice. Of course if Jo in accounts points out a factual inaccuracy or a spelling mistake just before you launch the video, then it may well be worth giving him or her a bonus.

A relevant example of this, from the highest echelons of power, was revealed in a scholarly study of the 2012 US Presidential Election's use of social media (published by the academic Daniel Kreiss in late 2014). Barack Obama's digital team was sleek in number, had access to decision-makers and was fleet of foot in being able to issue Tweets and other social media messages. But his rival Mitt Romney's team needed between *17 and 22 different people* to authorise every single Tweet before it was published. It's not why Romney lost the election, but it didn't portray him as a President-in-waiting who was in touch with the general public. This sort of behaviour isn't limited to political campaigns, however: there are plenty of examples of digital agencies who spend so long creating tweets with corporate customers that they end up with bland, catch-all and please-few messages. Figure out a way to make your feedback process as fleet-of-foot as possible.

IT'S NOT AS HARD AS YOU THINK TO MAKE YOURSELF A MARKET LEADER

The buzzwords in online marketing in 2014 and 2015 were 'Content Marketing'. Many experts in the field believe that good, strong and relevant content is now far more important than traditional SEO. And there is a logic behind it: why spend large amounts on SEO only to have potential customers or clients arriving at your website only to then leave immediately. What is there for them to see? (Not to mention that you are almost exclusively relying on Google's algorithmic whims: you may be top of the tree one day and hung out to dry the next).

The answer, according to content marketing gurus, is to create enough information on your site that will make users not only hang around, but come back again and again. And they might even recommend you to other potential customers. What's not to like? With most estimates stating that there are over two billion Google searches per month, why aren't you providing just a few of the answers?

Several companies have already taken the initiative and are ramping up their offering. This goes way beyond just having a Twitter or Facebook feed embedded on the page. This is content that the consumer wants, is interested in, finds relevant and will appreciate.

Let's say, for example, that a regular golf player has a wrist injury. They play once or twice a week and are worried that the injury is going to set them back for the season. Being avid golfers who don't want this to happen, they are likely to Google for protective wrist-wraps that may either allow them to play or speed up the progress of their injury. Typically this might lead them to Amazon or similar, or in some cases to third party websites selling protective wrist gear.

Now, for the sake of the argument, let's imagine you are a company that produces exactly what our imaginary customer wants. You will undoubtedly employ some form of SEO to lure potential clients. But what experience will these potential customers have when they arrive? How much better would it be if they could find relevant information that pertained to them and their specific injury. All it might take would be to have a specialist blog about golf wrist injuries (perhaps written by an expert in the field, or someone on your staff if they have the expertise). Or, even better, what if there was short video about wrist injuries and golf, which offered tips on what to do and promoted your product?

That's where content marketing comes in.

Of course, where there's a trend, there's a backlash, and the notion of 'Content Shock' has come into play since the writer Mark Schaefer blogged about it in 2014 and 2015. In his blog, Schaefer looked at the economics of Content Marketing, and claimed it was not a sustainable financial model: there is a finite number of people who are looking to consume content, and they are not looking to consume every single piece of content out there. As a result, the argument goes, only the very best content has any chance of success, and this is much more likely to come from deep-pocketed large organisations who have the finances to swing a bat enough times until they hit a home run.

However, as plenty of commentators have pointed out, this really *should* be the case: the best content should always win out, be it on TV, the New York Times' bestseller list, or indeed, online video.

Just because more and more people are making short online video, it doesn't mean the market is totally saturated: the cream will still rise, and better videos and trends in video help to make the overall quality better.

NOBODY LIKES A SCOPE-PUSHER

A scope pusher is someone who commissions a video for £2,000 and expects the final product to look like it cost £200,000. While it's important to maximise the amount of material you film and make your final product look as good as possible, scope-pushing isn't a good thing. If you've worked with your production house properly, understood your budget correctly, looked at any pre-production images where necessary, then you should already have a good idea of what the final product will look like. That's not to say you shouldn't keep a close eye on all aspects of the production, and query it where necessary, but an overbearing and unrealistically demanding presence during production and post-production doesn't help anyone, and can often hamper proceedings. Scope-pushers gain reputations, and they are not usually good ones.

TAGGING/METADATA/VIDEO SITEMAPS

Ensure that you have all of this covered. It's not tricky, and it's not that time-consuming. But having spent the time and money to make a video, you need to make sure it's being picked up by at least Google (so you'll need to set up a sitemap – very easy to do and usually requires little more information than the URL/keyword description/duration/player location etc etc). Tag your video in your YouTube channel (you do have a YouTube channel, right?) with all the relevant keywords – it's all there and laid out for you in the edit section. Give your video as much potential visibility as possible.

If your video is being read correctly by Google, then it has a good chance of ranking highly in the search results page. As Google now blends in results from websites, blogs, news feeds, Twitter feeds and videos, and displays them all in its page rankings, you'll probably have noticed that videos are given thumbnails on these results pages. And eye-measuring technology has shown that users are drawn to video thumbnails on these results pages: with the right metadata and tagging then this could be *your* video. Video that scores highly in Google's view of what is being socially shared is also boosted on the search results' ranking page, so it's a positive circle: put the correct measures in place for your video to be found and shared and, as long as it is any good and is actually shared, the chances of it rising up the search results will be higher.

And there's a very easy trick which will help increase the number of people who view your videos enormously. It's a simple idea, and one which uses Google and YouTube search results to tell you not only which videos to make, but what to call them. Let's take an example and imagine you are in the wallpapering business (you might produce wallpaper, the paste that is used, instruct people how to wallpaper or some other related service). You can type into the YouTube search box the beginning of any term connected to your business, such as 'How to wallpaper...' and then immediately see what people are searching for. If you have related videos, or want to make related videos, then you can title them accordingly and see your overall number of views increase. But make sure that your videos are honest and fully respond to their title - nobody likes to be cheated and find a video that says one thing when it promises another. If you gain a reputation for having videos that are short, sharp and very much to the point, then your chances of creating returning viewers can only increase.

IS YOUTUBE'S HOME PAGE A DISASTER?

There is a school of thought that says yes, it is, and that YouTube has never quite figured out its homepage. It can be perceived as messy, unintuitive, unsure of its identity and usually dominated by an ad. Whether this is the case or not, it's certainly true that the page lacks a look that gives it a mainstream identity akin to the Google homepage, a LinkedIn profile page or a Facebook page (all of which undergo frequent subtle changes but are easy to conjure up in your mind's eye). When was the last time you actually discussed anything you saw on YouTube's homepage? In all likelihood, it's never happened.

Yet it remains the world's biggest online video site, and has seen off any pretenders to the throne as if it were swatting flies. But the curious anomaly about YouTube is that it doesn't make any money for its owner, Google. It does have a revenue in the low billions, but when offset against costs, it's more or less breaking even. According to some industry experts, most people don't watch videos on the site itself: instead they watch them as embeds on other sites. YouTube tends to refute allegations like this, and swerves the conversation to the latest round of original content that it has commissioned.

What this means – the constant announcement of new programming – is that there is an ongoing thirst for content. This doesn't only come from YouTube either: plenty of organisations want to muscle in on the act of owning what they like to call 'killer' content. This isn't likely to change too much in the near future. So if you can figure out how to make worthwhile content that does better than break even, then there are plenty of opportunities out there. But getting it on the homepage of YouTube may not be all that it is cracked up to be.

MOBILE

Mobiles are more than just phones. They are the ultimate time-filler, and video is perfect for the medium. And although only 33% of users currently see their mobile as the most important device with which to access the internet, all the signs indicate that mobile use is on its way to overtaking traditional desktop or even laptop use: more and more people prefer to use their mobile than their computer once they have left the office. In this still-early era of second-screening, the second screen that someone is using is far more likely to be a mobile device than a laptop. I notice this all the time now, and especially when I am watching films that are only a few years old – when they depict characters at home on a sofa casually using a laptop, it already seems to be out of date. The whole phenomenon of mobile is growing so quickly– so much so that some reports suggest that 'professional' videos will be watched nearly two thirds of the time on mobile devices by 2016. 3g/4G/EE Networks are going to make mobile videos the norm.

This needs to be borne in mind in a number of ways – and especially from a practical point of view. The days when filmmakers had to make sure their films were 'safe' for TV screens have now become the days when films need to be thought of in terms of how they will play on a phone. Make sure everything is legible and audible. Always make sure you have uploaded the right version. And always, *always* ensure that you watch the final product on a mobile screen before it is released to the world – you'll be surprised what you might suddenly notice that you would not see on a larger screen. Always try as hard as possible to put yourself in the place of the consumer by looking at the final product in the same way as he or she will.

A huge benefit to companies whose videos are being watched on mobile is that most users tend to watch them full-screen – which means they are devoid of ads and other on-screen distractions. If you capture someone's attention on mobile therefore, you're arguably likely to have *more* of that attention than you otherwise would.

INTERVIEW: BEN PIEARS

Ben Piears has had nearly 20 years digital media experience, and currently is Director of Content at the leading fashion brand Asos.com. I wanted to talk to him specifically about product videos, as Asos has an impressive record in this field.

Firstly Ben talked about some general thoughts he had regarding online video and companies:

I think one of the most often told anecdotes relating to online video is that someone senior in an organisation, at some point, says the words, "we should make more video".

A lot of the time, it's borne out of a desire to keep up to date, to show innovation and modernisation. It might be without any thought of why you should do this, just that you should. Because everyone else is. "And that's the future!" The same thing happened with social media. "We need a Facebook page" or "we need a LinkedIn page". Often the people asking are so senior that colleagues fear to ask the question, "Why?"

It's not to say you shouldn't make videos, but it's surprising how easy it is to mess it up. The question we all ask with content is 'What is the best way to present it?' It's tempting to go with the flashiest format available, but not always the right thing to do. Sounds obvious of course.

Video lends itself better to some themes and features better than others, but it can be expensive and sometimes complicated for large organisations when it comes to rights, production and hosting.

PH: Ben reflects some of the ideas I have already discussed – the 'let's make a viral!' idea, the fear factor that is often present in companies that leads to bad decisions being made (or at least no questioning of decisions that are made), and the need for companies to really think about what they are doing with their video, and why – especially vis-à-vis rights and budget.

Q: What lessons do you think anyone considering commissioning video might have learnt from this first era of online video?

BP: Getting people to watch the video you have made is, of course, hardest of all. YouTube offers a wide array of videos. And unless you're determined in your search, it's unlikely people want to invest more than 1 or 2 minutes on a clip. The rise of Vine, the popularity of gifs, all play to the short form content appetite.

And when matters of cost, speed of turnaround and resource come in, it's really easy to start creating content lacking the quality that your brand demands. All of a sudden, content budgets that delivered hundreds of news stories a month, now could only afford five or ten original videos in the same time period.

With the downturn in traditional advertising formats like banners, MPUs (mid-page units) and so on, and the increased demand and yield in video advertising, it meant that video content was now a necessity, so virtually overnight sites were covered in video players. The clamour for revenue meant that quality suffered, with just a few sites having the foresight or freedom to develop and evolve the format.

PH: This is really one of the key takeaways of both this interview and the book itself. It's not just a question of 'if you make it, they will watch' but more 'you have to make it really good, and something people will want to watch'. There is no point in just crowding your site with content that nobody wants to watch.

Q: How important do you think product videos are? In general and in terms of online fashion?

BP: Online shopping is a fact of life now, but one of the few potential barriers to buying clothes online is that the experience lacks the physicality of bricks and mortar outlets.

The touch and feel of the garment, trying it on, seeing how it hangs, these sensations can to some degree be addressed by video. Right now, it doesn't replace the usual product listings, but it can work well in tandem and offer a view of the clothes that's not possible with flat imagery. Video is hugely important in terms of extending your brand's voice to the audience, keeping them engaged and encouraging them to shop. Shoppable videos are now a staple of many e-commerce organisations, developing the format so that it can be aspirational and practical.

PH: This of course begs the question of how much this all costs: how do you factor in the cost of creating product videos while at the same time keeping your own product prices as competitive as possible?

Q: What is the process? Do you have an in-house team or do you commission it externally? What have you learned along the way in terms of making the process as effective as possible?

It depends. At some places that are large enough, and with enough faith in investing in the content, an in-house team of video producers is required. More often than not they are all-rounders, often coming from a background of camera work, but with editing skills as well. Equipment and resources get bigger and bigger very quickly though and before you know it, the video team and its equipment is huge.

The only reason you would have this in-house team is if you are committed to making video content on a regular basis, otherwise it doesn't work.

And even if you outsource a great deal of your video content to other providers, most big organisations will have an in-house video expert (akin to one of the all-rounders above) to deal with assets as they come in, check rights and hosting and so on. Even if you have an in-house team, one-offs and sudden increases in output mean you always end up using an external source at some point too, but for prolonged content it might make better sense to bring it in-house.

It's also very important to understand where you want your video hosted, where it will predominantly sit and other rules around it. Too often sites seem to want it hosted solely on their website, but this seems to be disappearing as people wake up to the power of YouTube and bringing the content to the people and not the other way round.

Storyboarding and scripting it well in advance is a necessity, as are occasional dry runs. Finding locations to shoot in is of course crucial, and particularly with fashion, absolutely vital in creating the right atmosphere and scene you want to portray.

PH In a nutshell Ben has outlined the many varied and complex factors that are needed if a company is considering frequent video productions – and a lot of the time many of these factors are ignored.

Q: How do you factor in the cost?

BP: There's a fair bit of trial and error at first, and with video, it seems par for the course that you underestimate the time and people it takes to get what you want.

Q: How do you decide which items should be filmed?

BP: It entirely depends on the shoot and what it is you're trying to do.

Q: How do you push the videos to consumers? How important is social in all of this?

BP: Crucial. Particularly if you are pushing content that isn't purchase-orientated. Many videos will be simply content extensions of the brand. There's an argument to say these shouldn't be sat on the e-commerce site at all as, particularly with guys, they have come to shop. Again, best to target them where they expect to consume this type of content.

If the content is to help them buy, then yes it can be sat alongside product, but again, YouTube is still the best bet in getting people to view it. As are the usual social channels to promote it.

Social is important yes, but only if you use that social media to push content similar to this.

Q: How do you measure the success of the videos (metrics, click attribution etc)?

BP: Plays, shares, comments, click throughs if it's clickable / shoppable. It all depends what the goals are for that content. If it's engagement in terms of brand, then possibly views and shares (but is a guy likely to share a piece of fashion-related content?).

Q: What other ways can retailers use videos, or what other examples have you worked on (Challenge Asos for example)?

BP: As mentioned above, campaigns to heighten awareness of a product or a trend can be used. These are more aspirational or even left-field, trying to convey a mood and style rather than be practical and "buy this". With Challenge Asos we aimed to highlight the range of denim on the store, but not in a "buy this buy it now!" way. We chose a more humorous angle to appeal to guys, and less about the fashion element without it being uncool.

PH: There are several key things from my interview with Ben that have popped up elsewhere in this book: firstly the notion that companies often underestimate just how complex the process is in creating product or demo videos, and the effect on time and budget. Then there's the 'fear factor', something we have mentioned multiple times, whereby ideas from senior figures (who may not know that much about video/social media) are accepted without being challenged or properly examined. The importance of YouTube compared to videos being hosted on a company's website is still something that isn't fully accepted, while the importance of setting goals – be they to achieve a defined number of click-throughs or sales, or just to raise some general awareness – is essential in any marketing project, be it video-related or not.

IT'S NOT ALL ABOUT YOUTUBE

It's not always just about getting your video on YouTube and hoping for millions of views (in fact, as a strategy, just putting it out there and sitting back is probably the worst thing you can do). There are more and more sites and services offering a number of innovative ways for you to use video. Many companies now have accounts set up on one or all of the services below, and there's a growing industry for the likes of Vine or Instagram specialists.

<u>Vine:</u> Launched in January 2013, Vine is owned by Twitter and the intention is to make it Twitter for the short-form video world. Anyone can upload a video they have filmed themselves on their mobile phone or equivalent. The subject can be anything (taste and decency permitting: Vine soon found itself in the headlines for showing age-restricted content) but the caveat is that videos can be a maximum of 6 seconds long. Doesn't sound very long does it? But a quick peek at the Vine feed shows that most people have adapted to the new 6-second rule quite easily. In under a minute, watching the Vine feed, you can be transported to the tunnel of a sports stadium just as the team are about to take to the pitch, a boardroom in Tallinn, or a geography lecture in Pretoria. With no barrier to entry – it's free and everyone can make their own 6-second film now – there are myriad possibilities for companies here. And it doesn't have to be one single 6-second take, it can be any number of images that add up to 6 seconds. So why not check it out? You could make a 6-second day in the life of your company. A 'how we make our product' short. Or highlight some of the fun things you do. More and more companies are making their Vine mark.

Vine's success in 2013 made it an essential and cheap tool: soon after its launch, it had overtaken Instagram in terms of app download figures (although the two played ping pong over the course of the year at the top of the download chart). It resulted in Instagram rush-releasing its own short-form video app, whereby users could upload up to 15 seconds of film.

This happened in June of 2013 and **Instagram** video was immediately seen as the new competitor on the block: arguably because of its dominance in the image world, it was assumed by onlookers that this would naturally transfer into the very shortform video market. Soon enough, commentators were proclaiming this to be the case: as brands moved in and took advantage of the new platform by the end of 2013, Instagram Video was being hailed as major player. But the reality is, in fact, somewhat different. A year on from its launch, videos on Instagram account for only around 1% of all socially shared videos, probably because users are less likely to share overtly promoted 'brand Instavideos'. Yet don't dismiss Instagram too easily: it is, after all, owned by Facebook so complements the social network, and its userbase went through a significant increase in 2014 and has continued to do so in 2015. And depending on which measurement you take into consideration, Instagram is even ahead of Twitter in certain metrics (although in terms of sheer reach and shareability, Twitter still dominates).

But there is a purity and simplicity about Instagram which is making it more and more attractive to users. There isn't the noise of Twitter or the pressure to perform sometimes associated with Facebook.

Slideshark: Slideshark is a pretty nifty way of putting your PowerPoint presentations online for the world to see. You can embed hyperlinks as well as video and it's a useful consideration for anyone wanting to show some more complex information about your company, for example at an earnings call. I've also got a soft spot for Prezi, which is a fairly dynamic presentation tool that also allows video embedding. Another tool in this sphere is Brainshark, which is targeted at offering companies the chance to get low cost and very quick videos out to their staff. Spreecast is also well worth looking at in terms of broadcasting to a mass online audience.

Snapchat: Much written about (and the origin and continuing drama of the Snapchat founders' story is well worth checking out), Snapchat was based on an idea that very few outside of the originators thought would work: users could share photos which would then be deleted after a specified amount of time (usually under 10 seconds). But by late 2014, over 700 million images were being shared *daily*, and Snapchat had introduced the facility to leave short video messages which would also disappear. Snapchat's core user base remains the teen market, which makes it a magnet for companies who want to target a younger audience. But they have to be very careful, as talking down to teens on a teen service can be akin to being an embarrassing Dad figure. Instead, wiser companies have realised that the best way to benefit from Snapchat is to sponsor an already active user for a period of time. Just like a Twitter takeover, a Snapchat Takeover can bring a decent amount of attention from a highly sought-after market.

Fora.TV: Nobody has ever recommended me to watch anything on Fora.TV, and I don't know why. (But then again, nobody's ever recommended me to read anything on the question and answer site Quora, one of my Top 5 online destinations, and I don't know why that is the case either.)

Fora.TV is pretty simple: they put up films and videos from conferences. Like TED, but specific to the kind of conference you might actually get sent to once in a while. Whatever your thing, there's probably a video of some kind about it on Fora. Education, social media, politics, business, science and tech are all covered. And whatever your field, you'd probably boost your knowledge considerably if you watched one or two videos a week on there. It does have a pay model, but the good people at Fora have put quite a lot of content on there for nothing.

It's also a great potential home for any conference video you might create yourself, and as a result a potentially very useful way of advertising your services.

Magnify.net: The explosion in content provision in the last few years has meant that there is an astonishing number of videos out there. An increasingly popular notion is the idea of video curation: whereby companies can host videos which may be very specific to their niche, or which will be of interest to potential customers, on their site (and try to become a content marketing hub as discussed). Magnify.net is an example of a site that will take care of the curation for you: they service hundreds of companies with exactly the type of video they might be looking for.

Google Hangouts: When Google scaled back its Google+ social network in the middle of 2015, there were few tears shed. 'Google had bitten off more than it could chew', we were told. 'It could never compete with Facebook'. However, Google's own instant message and video chat platform – Hangouts - has proved popular with those who use Google Plus (which is arguably the most underrated social network out there). It has some excellent features, especially in the group video area, whereby up to 10 users can get involved in a video chat. Once Google have simplified the offering to make it appealing to a broad consumer and company base, it could still have enormous potential.

VHX: It may be be that you have created content that is so good, or potentially so useful to a number of people, that you decide it might be worth selling. You could consider making DVDs, but that involves the headache of manufacture and physical distribution, and feels old-fashioned now (although don't dismiss DVDs completely – there is still a role for them). So why not consider a digital platform for this: services such as VHX allow you to sell directly to your audience. Plenty of comedians, for example, have taken the route of filming their own live shows and selling them directly to fans.

Twitch: If you want to see the extraordinary power of video games, and just how massive the younger market for them is, then head on over to Twitch for a few minutes, where you can watch people play video games while other people commentate on them. It might seem niche, but the site was bought by Amazon in 2014 for just short of 1 billion dollars.

Google Glass: The news that Google glass was being decommissioned came as something of a surprise in early 2015, but not to anyone who had been following its progress closely. Seen as the next big thing in 2013, the heat quickly cooled on Glass, the search engine's hugely touted optical wearable tech that set the internet alight as soon as Sergey Brin was spotted wearing them for testing purposes on the New York underground. The reasons it didn't taken off are manifold and complex – the slowness to market, the failure to capture the zeitgeist, concerns over potential health and security issues - but it's likely that some form of wearable optical tech will take off. To what degree remains to be seen, but it's worth bearing in mind as a potential outlet or mechanism. In some ways, Google Glass was overtaken in 2014 by the popularity of GoPro cameras, and the arrival of drones, which both give unusual, novel and unique visual perspectives. It's an age-old occurrence: the 'next big thing' being overtaken by a previously unheralded competitor that has a related, but ever-so-slightly different USP.

Apps: The apps market is so fluid and energetic that new applications are being launched every week. Many of them use video, and while it may be hard to figure out which ones will stick around, it's worth considering how video-based apps might benefit a company. One example might be to take an app such as Directr – which allows users to mix in their own videos and images and then gives it all a professional looking polish – and ask users or fans to create their own stories or videos about your product. Knovio is another example that launched in 2014, and allows users to add visuals and explanation by way of a webcam to a Powerpoint presentation. This does – as with any other campaign - need to be integrated into your overall plan, as otherwise it can be the app equivalent of having the 'lonely' YouTube channel. There are constant innovations in the apps world and the online video world, and companies that use innovative new technologies often find themselves gaining press attention. Another example in early 2015 was the onset of 3-D YouTube videos, which allowed users to drag around the screen for a more immersive video experience.

SOME POTENTIAL VIDEO IDEAS FOR YOUR WEBSITE

If you're struggling for inspiration for your next company video, why not try one of these?

Introduce the board. Most corporate websites have an 'About us' section which typically will introduce members of the board or members of management. Why not have a short video introducing them? It would give them a more human appeal. If you decide to do this make sure it is compartmentalised for each person in case of staff changes. But try not to make it boring and likewise avoid the 'wackiness' factor. If you're really feeling brave you could do it in the style of a TV or movie trailer or similar.

Webinar: Does your company specialise in a certain area? Or are you entering a new field and would like to be seen as a player or an authoritative voice which others should take note of? Then why not try a webinar? As we've already seen the tools are at your fingertips for you to invite and host any number of speakers to speak on a certain subject. We are very used to attending conferences on expensive tickets – this no longer needs to be the case: you can even host your own using video streaming services, with your branding there as a reinforcing tool. Imagine hosting a conference for people from all over the world with expert speakers from several companies, all under your umbrella? Spreecast is a perfect tool for doing this.

Infographics In 2010/2011 it was hard to spend too much time on the internet without coming across an infographic. Simply put, these are visually stimulating ways of showing numerical information which might otherwise be hard to get across. While their day in the sun as a stylistic tool may have waned due to overexposure, they can, with careful selection, still serve a purpose, and they do still have an appeal: many people learn visually and providing difficult statistical information in a fun format can be rewarding. In particular, if you operate in a niche area, they can have a viral aspect to them as they can often prove useful to fellow companies (in which case always make sure that your name/logo/branding is embedded in a way that competitors cannot claim it as theirs). Be warned that they do take time to get right, though, and can involve quite a lot of detailed work with an animator/graphic designer.

YOUR OWN TV CHAT SHOW

It could be argued that there is no such thing as a niche any more - or at least that everyone operates in their own niche. But even if you operate in a sector which seems on the face of it large – for example healthcare, oil, or mining – you are still likely to inhabit a niche within that section: *a specific area* of healthcare, oil or mining. You may not see other people from other companies in your sector every day, but you contact them or read about developments in your field through the now traditional means – email, websites, newsletters, trade magazines and so on. If your company is trying to make a name for itself in its field then it needs to stand out – and there are more ways than ever of doing this (having a robust, engaging and conversational Twitter feed is a simple and cost-effective starting point).

Combined with the above, there has also been an explosion in the popularity of knowledge-based media. Particularly in the last few years, as specialist information is within easy reach: with Wikipedia leading the way, solid, user-led websites like Quora have become information mainstays and TED talks have brought an air of cool excitement to the formerly dry world of information/education. (You can pay marketing experts a lot of money to learn that they call this kind of thing 'content marketing' or even a 'value exchange'.)

As the video age grows, possibly no other organisation has captured the growing desire for information more than TED. TED (which stands for Technology, Education and Design) is a non-profit organisation that actually started in the 1980s, but which has taken massive advantage of what the digital age has to offer. With over 1500 speeches available – for free – online, it hit a landmark figure of 1 billion views in 2012.

With excellent branding, frequently changing content and a menu that offers something for everyone, TED is the go-to site for speeches and discussions on zeitgeisty topics of the day. In a way, TED is the quintessential joy-bringer: making people feel better about themselves by giving them videos that once might have seemed the privilege of the educated elite. With world-quality speakers available at the click of a button, it's no surprise that TED has become a widely shared video phenomenon: barely a day goes by without someone posting a TED talk on my Facebook page, and it's something that I usually try to make the time to watch.

Other organisations have also tried to muscle in on this new information-friendly era, and video is an integral part of their offering. Education itself has also been visible in this space: the prevalence and popularity of massive online educational courses, whereby the likes of Stanford University offer versions of their courses to the public, online and for free, has meant that they need to use video in different ways: whether it be offering replays of speeches direct from the lecture hall, bespoke videos made by a professor on his or her smartphone, to classes made up of students from around the world discussing their latest assignment using a video service such as Google Hangout.

So why not get your own piece of the action? Why not become your own version of TED?

One area which has become particularly interesting for our clients is our 'panel show' discussion broadcasts. In short, these are web-based programmes, usually not longer than half an hour, in which a small group of experts discuss an issue of the day in a certain field. So if your particular healthcare speciality is the knee, then why don't you get your company to fund a panel show in which a group of people in the field discuss the key points of the day in knee conditions, surgery or the future of knee-related medicare. It doesn't have to be an ad for your company or services (in fact, it shouldn't be an ad for you) but it can discreetly have your key art in the background, have opening and closing titles which clearly show your company is behind it, and even an onscreen logo for the duration. This is now all a lot cheaper than you might imagine, and it's also quite easy to get guests: there are many competent speakers in each field who are happy to give up an hour or so of their time in order to have a credit like this.

This niche programming is unlikely to get you millions of views – but that is not the point. The real win here is that the *quality* of views is so high. The weight of viewer sentiment is so strong that you can instantly mark yourself out as a player/authority/leading figure in your field.

FURTHER THOUGHTS ON DISTRIBUTION

With so much content begging for attention, the importance of having a distribution plan cannot be underestimated. Other methods you can consider for your distribution plan include:

Hiring a distribution company. But there are plenty of caveats here.

Years ago, when I was a student actor at the Edinburgh Fringe, my show was one of 3,000 competing for the attention and cash of the visiting crowds. In an attempt to bolster ticket sales and publicity, we hired a flyer company to post our posters all over the city. But there were several problems: as soon as our posters were put up, another company came along and stuck their posters over them. With 3,000 shows screaming for attention, the very value of the posters became questionable. The big posters, owned by the big spaces and companies with deep pockets, seemed to have prestigious locations and more of an impact than our relatively small budget would allow. And finally, in what became the nail in the coffin of the whole poster story, one of our crew found several thousand of our posters dumped in an alley.

This isn't an allegory aimed at tarnishing the reputation of every online distribution company. But be wary before you part with your hard-earned cash to someone who promises you the Earth. They are, after all, representing you, and the manner in which they communicate may have a direct effect on your own reputation. What if, horror of horrors, they were 'buying' views to boost your count? You could end up with thousands of false leads which would completely negate the purpose of the exercise (I recently heard of a very experienced marketer who fell for such a scam, so it can happen to even the wisest of heads). If you are considering hiring a distribution company, it's essential to meet them face-to-face in order to get a feel for how exactly they will send out your video, and it's also a very good idea to have a detailed plan set up that you can monitor. And if it all works out successfully, then you've found yourself a strong partner for the future.

If I had to repeat my Edinburgh experience now, I would probably put all of the marketing budget into PR. And *hiring a PR company* for your video isn't quite as crazy an idea as it seems. The gateholders of the large platforms or websites are well-used to all sorts of pleas and attempts to get their attention and publish third party content, so specialist PR companies who understand the marketplace, have good contacts, and know when and where to place videos serve a useful purpose. There is even a selection of online tools which now promise to help you spread the PR word.

Sponsoring content or buying ad space such as on the pre-roll before the main video can also guarantee views, but as we have discussed elsewhere, the potential to annoy the audience is also quite high. I don't dismiss Paid Promotion completely, but its values do need to be weighed up carefully. Simply put, it's just so much more effective if your content earns its place: if getting picked up by a major media outlet is the gold standard, there are plenty of other ways that are also effective. Being hosted on an influential blog, advocate or trusted partner can have a hugely significant impact.

It's also worth having the right person in your network following the right set of contacts in your field: not just from an expertise point of view but also from a networking perspective. You never know when you might just have the right piece of content that an influencer will need.

TO GEO-BLOCK OR NOT TO GEO-BLOCK?

In late 2015 and early 2016, Netflix made headlines for the wrong reasons. It was apparently restricting users from watching it in countries where it did not officially have a service. It turned out that millions of people across the world were viewing Netflix via a VPN (Virtual Private Network). Netflix, which had neither a service in countries like Australia, nor the rights to show any programmes there, simply decided to stop them from viewing. As a paid up member of Netflix UK, I've used a VPN (Tunnel Bear) to access Netflix US myself, as the range of films and TV series is a little broader than the UK offering.

When this story broke, it presented Netflix with a thorny problem, and it's one that resonates across anyone who is launching even a simple video. Netflix pays content owners and creators a lot of money for the rights to broadcast their shows. Rights are often complicated, with multiple parties across multiple territories being involved. They are usually negotiated for periods of time, such as 18 months or a couple of years. That way the rights holder can maximise their profit, by offering evergreen content to different channels (or in this day and age, streaming services) for a number of years: once the rights are up with one service, they can begin a new run on another.

It was a fairly open secret that people could watch Netflix, or any other streaming service, with the aid of a VPN even in countries where the service was not up and running. I know several people who did, and still do, watch that way. The major reason it was tricky for Netflix was because it was accruing millions of views from countries where it shouldn't have been available, and all of these views when added to the bottom line made Netflix look like the market leader.

The story emerged into the public, then died down. Netflix denied that it was stopping anyone from watching its service using a VPN (I myself had a few unexplained interruptions while watching Netflix US around this time). But you can be sure that behind the scenes Netflix began having some very serious conversations with its content partners about exactly how their product was being exploited. If you own the Australian rights to a film, for example, and a million people watch it through an 'illegal' VPN, then clearly the value of those rights will plummet.

It's a Catch-22 for services such as Netflix, and raises the ghost of illegal downloading services such as Napster. Netflix subscribers, on the other hand, will probably protest that they pay for the service as a whole, so why shouldn't they receive the same product as viewers in another country?

On a related note, several large US TV comedy and chat shows have taken differing approaches to the ability to show clips from the shows in other territories. Networks such as NBC seem to take a scattergun approach: clips from certain shows such as Saturday Night Live are often geo-blocked in countries outside the United States, while the likes of Jimmy Fallon and Jon Stewart (who embraced the power of viral video in their respective roles of hosting The Tonight Show and The Daily Show) have been proactive in pushing their clips all over the web.

So if you are releasing a video, it's worth considering whether or not you need to geo-block it for any legal or rights-related reasons. It's more likely to be a question that will affect large corporate entities rather than small-scale releases, and in trying to figure out whether to let the world see your work or not, the answer should as much as possible be yes.

WHAT'S YOUR VIDEO *REALLY* ABOUT?

The best videos, like the best films, have layers. So much so that while they may appear to be about one thing on the surface, they may actually reflect something deeper on closer inspection. These are the types of video that can have lasting value. It particularly applies to topical, or social commentary videos: they might on the face of it seem to be about one subject, but they might actually be holding a mirror up to a certain group in society to reveal something new or unexpected.

This is a tricky area, namely because it is very hard to achieve. It's also full of potential pitfalls: companies who try to force certain issues to come to the fore may end up missing the point completely, with a final product that is neither one thing or another. It can also lead companies to stray into areas that they are not completely comfortable with, areas even that they shouldn't be involved with in the first place. This is particularly true about news-related videos – a lot of viewers will question why a company is getting involved in the first place.

A good, experienced writer is essential in such a project: one who is able to bring the nuances to the fore.

THE SMALL STORY

One of the most engaging pieces of corporate video I have seen in the few years were the 'Twitter stories' videos. These were beautifully produced examples of how the 'small story' can say so much about what a company does. They were so effective that I can remember one of them quite clearly without looking at it again (and I probably haven't seen it in about a year) – a struggling independent bookstore boosts its sales through a simple Twitter campaign involving the storeowner and his mother.

There were several impressive things about this film: it was beautifully shot, while remaining simple and classy. It did everything it needed to in under ninety seconds, most importantly of all explaining what Twitter does in a simple lightbulb way (despite its rapid rise, a lot of people still didn't know what the purpose of Twitter was in 2013). Most importantly, the makers realised that a small, personal story, told quickly, could highlight everything about the benefits of the product. (Which goes back to the age-old sales mantra that 'people buy from people').

What's your small story?

HOW OFTEN SHOULD I POST NEW VIDEO CONTENT?

There are different schools of thought on this subject. Some brands and organisations are picky with what they show and when they show it – they want to make the release of a new video a 'special' moment. Others prefer a more consistent approach, releasing new videos several times a week. This is reflective of the YouTube stars' approach: a lot of lo-fi content released very frequently (think of gaming star PewDiePie or make-up expert Grace Chan, who both release several videos a week). One company that 'releases' several videos a week is Lootcrate, a service that sends customers a regular box of cool new 'stuff'. The subsequent 'unboxing' videos by their users serve as part of the Lootcrate online visual experience.

As a rule-of-thumb, if you're going to release a *lot* of content, then you need to accept that some of it may be of lower production or creative quality. But that's not always a bad thing – think of the production values of the typical bedroom YouTube star. You may also not get a 'hit' every single time, which is something that you'll need to accept from the start. If you are making a higher end product, then you'll need to make sure that the marketing and PR and distribution is finely tuned before you release it.

It's worth underlining again that content doesn't need to be all video: it should be a mix of material which is visual (such as video or an image), audio (such as a podcast) and written (such as articles and blogs). Videos on their own won't usually work as a 'magic bullet' without more substance to back them up.

WHAT ARE THE KEY DRIVERS IN SHARING ONLINE VIDEO?

Sharing an online video is guided by a number of factors: emotion, perception, the brilliance of an individual video. And luck. The science of emotion in marketing is a complex and well-trodden subject, but let's take a brief look at each of these as they relate to viral video.

Emotion: This is probably the most important reason that a video is shared. *How does it make you feel?* And within the wide range of emotions that we all feel at different times of the day, happiness is by far the biggest driver in shareable videos. We talk about joy a lot in this book, but its importance cannot be underestimated in making a video shareable. Joy, amusement, delight: they are all key drivers in making something shareable. That's why comedy (making people laugh), children and animals all feature in many of the most highly shared videos. Sure, other emotions come into play in the scale of sharing (there is, for example, still a place for shock horror videos – if they are done correctly such as the Carrie video we discuss elsewhere. Fear is also high on the list of emotions that promote sharing). This also may account for the reason that the charity world finds it so tough to create videos that are highly shareable: because of the content matter (which people may see as something of a downer), viewers are unlikely to want to pass it along to their friends. Inspiring videos have a better chance. Awe-inspiring ones even more so. That's not to say charities should abandon the notion of making emotional videos completely: but these are much better used in a fundraising or call-to-action environment rather than a sharing one.

Emotion is also widely recognised as a key driver in decision-making: studies have shown that accident victims who have a diminished emotional side take a lot longer to make decisions than the average person. Therefore when it comes to a purchase-related decision, emotion is again hugely important: which is why videos aimed at making someone purchase will have a much higher impact if they tap into viewers' emotions.

But because people also think, and like to learn or be surprised, a video that successfully creates both an emotional and rational reaction may even stand a better chance of doing very well.

Of course anger is another strong emotion that can lead to online sharing – but it is usually aimed at antagonising (or being antagonised by) someone or something. Facebook feeds are increasingly full of outspoken commentary on world affairs. Associating with disgust or antipathy is probably not something a brand wants to do.

Perception: What does the kind of video you share say about you? We are 10 years into the Facebook age now, so people are a little more discerning when it comes to sharing video. They may have had the odd comment in real life from someone about a video they shared, which in turn may lead them to think twice about sharing the next time. They may not, for example, want to be pigeonholed into being 'that guy' or 'that girl' who always shares 'that kind' of video. So, as people have become accustomed to realising that what they share may say a lot about them, perception becomes more and more important. And this, in turn, may lead to the development of 'sharing fatigue': the notion that 'videos are so prevalent anyway, why should I bother to share this one', or 'if I share another video like this, what will people think about me?'

How is it shared? Nevertheless, as we have seen, people are much more likely to respond to a shared item if it comes from a person rather than a brand. Studies have been done on the open rates of tweets which come from a brand compared to those which are shared by an individual, and they show that tweets containing links which are sent by an individual have a higher open rate than tweets sent by brands. Of course, brands themselves need to share their content, but it's only when this content is deemed significant enough to be shared by individuals that it can really take off. So, personally shared videos on Facebook usually have a higher view-rate, as the audience has already bought in to the sharer (unless they are 'that guy' or 'that girl' as above. And email share rates, if sent by an individual to a small core group, can still be very strong. The key aim for companies in video is to both have a video that delivers the message in a way that's clever and engaging enough not to alienate their audience (or a new audience) and to magically infiltrate these core sharing groups.

Brilliance of an individual video: This is usually the once in a lifetime incredible moment that everyone in the world has to see right now. Felix Baumgartner's freefall onto the planet for example. These are rare beasts, the Holy Grail of shareability.

Luck: 'Charlie Bit My Finger' contains several of the above elements: it provokes a great feeling of happiness, it's funny, has children, and anyone who shared it was likely to be perceived as a kind-hearted or good-natured soul. But luck of course played a massive part: for the person to be there to film that moment at that particular time.

The Age and Sex of the Person Who Is Sharing: There are various studies into the breakdown of who is more likely to share a video? A female teen? A male 30-something? Studies show that there are a few groups that have higher sharing rates than others – but bear in mind that they are likely to be sharing *certain types* of video. Focussing on one group as a target may support your individual market interest, but it may also be easier said than done, and ignoring, or worse still, making certain groups feel excluded, may have a detrimental effect. However, there is evidence that while females are more active in actually sharing content, the content that they are sharing is more likely to come from a male account: there exists a social network gender bias, possibly because somewhere deep down in the male psyche there is a trigger that makes them less likely to share something that originated from a female-held account.

The overall trend of the types of videos that are shared is likely to change year-on-year: whereas a few years ago humorous videos led the way, the more emotional/joy-filled videos have more recently come to the fore. But it has to be genuine emotion and joy – as we have seen again and again, viewers will see through anything fake straight away.

LOS 33

In 2010, one of our first big viral hits was 'Los 33', our spoof film trailer about the plight of the 33 Chilean miners who were trapped below ground for 69 days as the world watched and prayed for their safe return.

It taught me two things. It gave me one of the first examples of the power of the celebrity retweet in helping a video to go viral, and it also opened my eyes as to how large media organisations and rights owners were beginning to show a different attitude to their assets being used in spoof videos on the web. In this case the celebrities were Stephen Fry and John Cleese, and the news network was America's ABC. And far from sending cease and desist letters, ABC embraced their appearance in the video and promoted it to the front page of their website.

It all began a few days before the miners were released from their underground prison. Watching the 24-hour news cycle we wondered to ourselves 'Who would play these guys in the inevitable Hollywood film of their story'? Brad Pitt? George Clooney? We started to laugh, and then we started to think that this could make a funny spoof film trailer. We featured topical footage from ABC's new broadcasts on the miners and we had a glittering cast of 33 actors to play the miners – everyone from Leonardo DiCaprio to Tom Hanks to Stephen Fry and Justin Bieber. And Meryl Streep. And Woody Allen. We spent quite a lot of time discussing whether or not Darth Vader should make an appearance but, wisely, left him out.

The release of our video coincided with the release of the miners: for a couple of days, the news cycle was so consumed with them that our film had a paltry number of views.

But then Stephen Fry discovered it. A Twitter follower of his had seen the video and sent it to him, simply saying 'Stephen, we didn't know you were going to be in the Chilean miners film'. Fry's interest was obviously piqued: he retweeted it, and the avalanche of views began. The comments below the video on YouTube started to come in, first at a trickle then literally at a rate of several per second.

Soon it was picked up by Twitter and Facebook (it had 20,000 Facebook likes in the first 24 hours after it went viral). Blogs featured it, and, because it was centred on a South American story, the press there went crazy for it. And ABC News in the United States, with its prominent role as the news 'broadcaster' in our film, took it to heart and proudly positioned it on their front page.

Of course what was true then may not be true now, especially in terms of the 'celebrity retweet'. People in the public eye who have a social network presence are much more savvy now and are actually less likely to retweet a video. They are undoubtedly being barraged every day by Twitter pranksters begging them to retweet the latest video or image. Of course, they still might – but the quality threshold is now somewhat higher than it was. You are likely to be dealing with a lot more competitors for their attention. One way that may grab their attention is if they feature in it, but you have to make sure that you are portraying them in a positive, friendly light. (The Chilean miners story was so big that Fry hopefully saw our video for what it was, an amusing reflection on it, and found it amusing that he might play one of the miners). If you are going to include a celebrity, then also you need to think about where you position him or her in the video. Fry was the 26th actor of the 33 we chose, so had to watch over three quarters of it to see himself. And we figured that featuring superstars who were unlikely to personally retweet might also yield extra views, as long as we could get to their fans: hence the legion of Justin Bieber fans who flocked to the video to see their hero positioned in 30th place in our list.

We didn't ask or pay to use any of the clips in this video. Yet the major international broadcaster who featured the most was happy to go with it, and none of the clip owners came after us. As we have seen, this isn't always the case, and it may be more acceptable to do this in a web format than it might be on television. But it was an indication of a growing sea-change in attitudes of these rights-owners.

QUALITY OF VIEWS VERSUS NUMBER OF VIEWS

There's an increasingly common idea among Twitter marketeers that the 'quality' of followers is more important than the number of followers. So 100 strong advocates (important and influential people in your field) might be worth more to you than 1,000 casual observers.

The same could be said of a short form video campaign. It all goes back to what your message is and who it is aimed at. While you might probably be thinking that the fundamental reason to have a video is to drive sales, there are times when this may take a back seat, (if, for example, you want to prioritise an awareness campaign). We did a very specific campaign for a client who was less concerned about the sheer volume of views than the quality of them (it was a call-to-action campaign for a niche new test initiative they were launching. They didn't have the set-up to deal with thousands of responses and enquiries but wanted to see if there was likely to be an initial uptake on their offering). Once the film was finished it was targeted at specific viewers on the client's database, and it was a perfect example of how a client was happier with 1,000 views rather than 10,000.

THE MORE TIME YOU SPEND ON KEYWORDS, THE BETTER THE RESULT WILL BE

There are myriad ways of measuring the success of a video. Pure views, percentage of shares, how long people stay on the video, whether they actually complete watching it, how many subscribers you have compared to your competitor etc.

But an important, if sometimes overlooked, factor is just how you get people to your video in the first place. The simple answer is that most people who are doing a search will use Google or YouTube, but it's not a widely known fact that even though they are owned by the same company, they do not have the same keyword algorithms. In short, the success of certain keywords to get people to your video from Google may not be replicated on YouTube. It's very important to pay attention to this, and to even consider some split-testing to see what works best for you. Seasonal fluctuations may also be a factor (people are more likely to search for deals in the run-up to Christmas and the New Year), and language differences (especially if your video is aimed at a very wide audience) also need to be borne in mind.

All of this, as well as creating content that will increase the time people spend watching your video as well as improving the quality of your metadata and having many distribution channels, will help to increase your ranking (status) on YouTube.

HOW DOES YOUTUBE DECIDE THE ORDER OF HOW IT DISPLAYS ITS VIDEOS?

Have you ever wondered how YouTube decides how to rank its videos in its search results? For a long time after the service started, this was done according to the view count of a specific video – it seemed logical that the most popular videos should be ranked at the top of the search results page. But then someone at YouTube realised that this might not be the best way of ranking videos. What if people were using artificial means of boosting a video's view counts? And what if the video itself wasn't that great, but was simply the victim of its own success due to its view numbers? If you take it to a logical conclusion, ranking videos simply according to number of views would mean that people would never get to see any new videos.

As a result, YouTube tweaked its system and gave a lot greater weight to 'time watched'. This, simply enough, is a measurement of how long people were sticking around on a particular video. If the video was good and relevant, they would keep watching until the end, and if not they would soon click away. You can look up the minutiae of this algorithm, but it basically boils down to how much time a user spends on a given video during their specific YouTube session.

The significance for video producers should be fairly obvious: keep people watching. And do this by *creating content that keeps people watching*. Don't try and cheat the system by weighing a long video with an all-important final 30 seconds, as this will be found out. But the rankings secret is just that – and isn't really a secret at all – keep making content that people want to watch. Simple, right?

Of course, YouTube still faces problems in its most important function (to get viewers the video they want to watch as quickly and easily as possible). There are many people out there using bots to mess with the rankings, and in terms of news videos, the most recent trend has been to create substandard news reports using robot voices – videos which anyone would click away from in a matter of seconds. It's worth keeping up with the trends of how people are trying to 'game' YouTube, in order to make sure your video isn't falling into this trap.

IS IT POSSIBLE FOR YOUR COMPANY TO HAVE *TOO MANY* VIDEOS ON YOUTUBE?

One of the big social sins that companies can commit is to over-communicate with their userbase. A constant stream of tweets and Facebook updates can be off-putting for people, especially if it is in the wrong tone, and can provoke them into quickly pressing the unfollow or block button. But the same doesn't really apply to YouTube. It's a less 'pushy' network, as it doesn't quite stream in the same way as Facebook or Twitter feeds.

There is no hard and fast rule for the number of videos you put out. A more important consideration is to make sure you have a steady flow of content: video should be part of an overall campaign which should usually consist of several pieces, and when the campaign finishes you should have some follow-up material ready. It's not hugely impressive when companies blitz a campaign for a period of time and, six months later, when viewers come across their YouTube page, there is nothing there.

While a steady flow of material is important, (it could be one video a week, or ten a month), there are situations when a lot of videos will help spread your message. This is particularly the case for any organisation that has a growing and involved community. Crafts or video gamers are good examples. Crafting users tend to be extremely communal: they are keen to show off their work, techniques and share tips. As a result there are plenty of examples of crafts where a lot of users have created their own video to show off their latest find or creation. Similarly, video gamers are very keen to both show off their highest scores, or to discover walk-throughs of the chapters of a particular game they may be stuck on.

It's well worth considering how you can harness individual users in order to spread your organisation's word. There are examples of topics that have thousands of videos, all generated by users. So when new fans come to search for the topic, they immediately see that there is an established core of users. It's important to remember that such growth needs to be organic, and generated by individuals/small groups, as opposed to having a top-down 'corporate' feel. Creating enthusiasm, sharing awareness and feedback are all ways of sharing engagement.

THE PROS AND CONS OF MOODBOARDS AND MOOD VIDEOS

If you've just commissioned a video, or you're about to embark on making a video for a company that has hired you, then you might consider creating a moodboard. This is usually a series of images which add together to convey the type of video you might make: its mood, style, visual inspiration and the like. It's often presented to clients to give an idea of what they might expect from the final product. Moodboards can often be a very good idea, and can form a big part of a pitch to win a commission in the first place.

But while moodboards have their place, mood videos can be problematic, and I generally advise avoiding them. A mood video is a more elaborate version of a moodboard: a short video which will give an outline of what the final product might look like. The main problem with moodboards is that prospective clients are often unable to understand that they are 'demos' for the final product. They may be quickly put together, a bit sloppy in appearance, but clients will often jump on them as examples of what the final product actually will be. They won't get that a few short hours' work to create a visual or storytelling 'look' are just that – a few short hours' work – and it can create unnecessary problems at a very early stage. So, while moodboards can be a help, mood videos can often be a hindrance. Note though, that mood videos are separate from test videos, which are often a very good idea: testing camera shots, visual graphics and rehearsing as much as possible is highly recommended.

PODCASTING: YOUR NEXT VIDEO STRATEGY

If you or your company have taken the bull by horns and have a strong and robust video strategy (which involves a comprehensive before and after delivery plan), then you are officially in the content business. Perhaps you are also commissioning articles in your field from authoritative figures. All of this is giving the wider world the impression that your website (or content hub) is a destination venue for valuable information about your area of expertise.

If this *is* the case, then you need to strongly consider podcasting. While podcasts have been around since the dawn of the internet era, they have undergone a massive spike in popularity in the last year/eighteen months. And this is only going to increase as people get more and more used to realising that there is a world of choice out there in terms of listening. There are now podcasts on pretty much any subject, and unlike video assets they do not require visual attention. This means that they are hugely popular with people who are on-the-go, whether it be as a download on their phone or, increasingly, in the car. Business people who are driving in the future will be doing so in vehicles equipped with web capabilities: and as well as choosing standard scheduled radio shows, the wide world of podcasts will be available to them.

We are not talking here about the podcasts issued by media organisations, which usually comprise of shortened versions of broadcast shows (and which, due to the inability of the legal system to keep up with changes, are only allowed to play brief sections of any music choices). These are a great way of entertaining yourself and catching up with your favourite shows.

What we are talking about are podcasts created by individuals about their specific niche area: be it flyfishing, arts and crafts, home improvement or even subsections of those subjects. No matter what field you operate in, it's highly likely that you have something interesting to say about it. And it's also highly likely that you know other experts in the field who would be only too happy to appear on your podcast as guests.

It's inexpensive and relatively simple to set up a podcast. All you really need is a decent microphone and some simple editing skills. There is already a burgeoning business in 'how to podcast' books and seminars, which will take you through the steps you need to create a series (or, ideally, a regular programme that always runs).

The upside is potentially tremendous. It shows clients, customers and potential customers that you are very serious about your subject, and a trusted source on the matter. This can only lead to an increase in interest in what you have to offer, and have an effect on your bottom line. What's more, the sponsorship and advertising possibilities available to podcasters are also growing: some of the figures that have been publicly discussed by the likes of hugely popular podcasters such as John Lee Dumas are eye-watering (Dumas reportedly makes hundreds of thousands of dollars *a month* from his business podcast). So – if your video strategy is robust, you need to seriously consider adding podcasts to your content arsenal.

IS A PICTURE WORTH A THOUSAND VIDEOS?

Not quite. But there are times when a well-crafted image *might* be better than a video. We've created hundreds of videos for clients over the last few years. But we've also probably delivered as many images, if not more.

Images have several potential advantages over video. They are quicker to make, so they are especially good if you want to react very quickly to an item in the news. By the time you've made a video, the news cycle may have moved on and all your hard work and expense may have been wasted. They are more quickly shareable and less fiddly: all someone has to do is to look at an image to decide if it is funny or interesting and if they want to share it or not. Successfully shared images can have hundreds of thousands if not millions of views.

On the other hand, images are easy to 'steal'. It's fairly common for widely shared images to have a life of their own as 'pirated' versions because, sadly, there are plenty of people who are happy to crop any logo or brand name out and pass them off as their own. They are also much more ephemeral than videos: it's much less likely, for example, to hear people ask 'Did you see that image?' as opposed to 'Did you see that video?' Images provide an instant hit, while videos offer a deeper, more substantial experience. And images are much more commonplace, so it's a lot harder to stand out.

If you are going to employ images as part of your viral strategy – and I highly recommend it – it's a good idea to have a top-of-the-range graphics artist in your team. Not just someone who can run off something on Photoshop. It's also important to bear in mind some image tips: simple images are more effective than complex ones (although complex comedic flowcharts are always popular), people don't like to be hoodwinked, so 'fake' images (ie purporting to be real ones) don't go down well, and always be extremely careful if you are using an archived image as part of your source: image galleries are notoriously litigious and chase after people who they believe to be using their product without the correct licence.

HOW MANY VIEWS MAKE A VIDEO AN 'INTERNET SENSATION'?

In the summer of 2015 I was interviewed for the popular Radio 2 Simon Mayo Drivetime Show as the 'expert' in the field of what makes a viral video come to be regarded as a viral video.

I watch an awful lot of viral videos, and an awful lot of them are called 'internet sensations'. This description seems to be especially used by traditional media, especially newspapers (and especially local newspapers when they are covering a locally-made video that has had an audience.)

But exactly how many video views make something an 'internet sensation'?

The answer is that there is *no* correct answer: it's all about perception. Sure, there are mega-blockbuster videos that have had hundreds of millions of views. These can justifiably be called 'internet sensations'. But I've also seen videos which have had 20,000 views given the same name, and I've made videos that have had 50,000 views which have been so described. The decision to label something an 'internet sensation' is very much a subjective thing. Of course, there are landmarks in the progress of a video: the first 10,000, 100,000 or million views, for example. But there is no hard-and-fast scale.

What it does mean is that if you are a video-maker (or a company that has commissioned a video) and something you have done is labelled an 'internet sensation' by an authoritative voice (which is most likely to be a traditional media outlet), then you should regard this as extremely useful free publicity, as well as a badge-of-honour and reference that you can show future clients.

ONLINE VIDEO'S DIRTY LITTLE SECRET: BUYING VIEWS

Did you know that the view counter underneath every YouTube video may not be telling the truth?

Not in terms of actual number of views. It's usually fairly accurate in this regard. But there exists a hidden world of viewer manipulation which is becoming an increasingly common business practice by corporate communication types desperate to prove to their bosses that the video they commissioned is being watched.

It's called buying views. If you Google 'buying YouTube views' you'll be given a wide selection of choices. Prices start from only a few dollars for 5,000 views. Is it the stuff of desperate measures, or a worthwhile method of drawing attention to your video?

In theory it could be useful: certainly if you've launched a video and want to show people that you have traction. It may even lead to an overall greater bump in your audience. But before you consider this option you need to think very carefully about a number of things.

Who will be watching? If this is all being done from a click-farm in Asia then you might have trouble assessing the *quality* of views you are getting. Successful online video is often about quality of views as much as quantity: hitting the right target group at the right time is generally the aim. 1,000 views from people who might be converted into solid leads is arguably much more worthwhile than 10,000 views from a bot: some of the 1,000 might, after all, turn into long term customers.

Are they actually watching? A lot of the companies that offer this service simply rent IP addresses in various parts of the world, and embed and automatically play the video once the website is viewed. But often the viewer will simply close the website after two or three seconds: meaning that the view count will say one thing while the actual views (retained viewers, or anyone who sticks around long enough to view the whole thing) will be almost minimal.

You'll probably be found out. If anyone in your company is tracking the analytics and they see a sudden unexplained spike from a certain country, or if they see views fall off the cliff once your buying period is over, it won't take them long to realise that something is afoot. The shame and difficulty in explaining is one thing: the effect on your career may be altogether more serious. More elaborate schemes exist to make it seem that the bulk viewing is coming from a number of countries and thus hide this fact but it is still, essentially, cheating. An easy way of checking out if a video's views are fake is to check the number of comments underneath it on YouTube – if a video has 500,000 views and only 3 comments for example, then something strange is going on.

What's the point? You may pull the wool over a few eyes for a short period of time, but ultimately it's a futile experience: one that's hard to explain when the truth is revealed.

But is it actively done by anyone? If it weren't then surely the businesses wouldn't exist. There are plenty of articles online saying that it's especially common in the music business, where for a cheap spend labels can boost their act's new release. This will not only make them appear successful or at least credible, the logic goes, but if a video hits a certain number of views, say 10 or

20,000, it has a much better chance of taking off on its own. It's ultimately a question of ethics as to whether you follow this path.

TOPICAL VERSUS SEMI-TOPICAL

If you are considering creating a video that relates to a topical aspect of the news cycle, it's essential to remember that all news stories have a limited life cycle. Today's hot topic will often be a distant memory in a week's time (or, increasingly, a day's time). We look at this in a little more detail in our analysis of our Topical video creation, but a key point is how to figure out how many resources you need to put into your Topical campaign. As we have seen it can be a time-consuming and resource-heavy engagement, so think carefully in terms of how this fits into your overall marketing spend.

To deal with ultra-specific time-sensitive campaigns of a Topical nature, we launched The Situation Room in early 2013. This is a specific part of our business that deals with urgent up-to-the-minute reactive video. It might be damage control: if a major marketing faux pas has taken place within your organisation, you might need to counter it by issuing rapid video responses. Or it might be that a news story has affected your industry: again a video on the subject can prove highly effective. It could even be a whim: an amusing or relevant idea which you feel you would love to put out there. It's this kind of instant reaction that could mark you down as a leading figure in your field.

Another notion that is worth thinking about is the idea of a campaign being 'semi-topical'. When we look at pressing the button on a new topical video, we not only think about its potential 'shareability', but whether it revolves around a generally topical story that will give it 'legs'. Semi-topical videos also work well around annual festivities or recurring events: Christmas, holidays, winter: these are all areas where a successful video can have more than one run.

One of the main issues with a video going viral is that its creators aren't prepared for the onslaught of opinion it will engender, and quite how to react to it. If you release something on a Friday and it has a million views over the weekend – some of them positive and some of them negative - do you have the sytems in place to react correctly? Can you capitalise on the sudden burst of interest in your brand or product? Have you prepared a follow-up, or will you end up being vaguely remembered as 'that company that did that thing'? Unless you have a solid follow-up plan and a willingness to be in the long game – trying to figure out content that will hit the spot again and again and again – you might want to consider the validity of entering the field in the first place.

And videos are more and more likely to get a reaction: unless they are so bland that they become invisible and part of the 'lonely YouTube channel'. Part of the reason for this is that as the internet has grown, more and more people feel like they must have an opinion. And they value that opinion very highly. Whereas in the 1990s and before, in the pre-mass internet era, people were likely to keep their opinions to themselves, and writing a letter to the paper was considered an unusual (or in some cases radical) act, today most web users feel they have the right to comment. The comments pages of online newspaper articles are, for example, often more fascinating than the article itself. And because people comment, and maybe even build up small followings themselves (say 10 or 20 thousand followers on Twitter) they may end up with an over-inflated sense of their own importance. Putting all of these people's opinions into some form of context, especially in relation to your brand, is a task that is still in its infancy.

POTENTIAL PITFALLS: DON'T HOG THE LIMELIGHT

One of the biggest flaws I see when watching company overview profiles on the front page of a website is too much information about the founder or founders, or their 'incredible journey' to where they are today. This is not the first thing potential customers should see. There *is* plenty of scope for it (assuming that it actually is interesting) but this should happen later on in the customer experience.

Once you have converted a customer then they may well be very interested in who you are and what your background is and how you came to launch your product. But the casual surfer, or the more qualified visitor who may be looking at your site and comparing it to several others before making a purchasing decision, wants to know what it is you do or sell and why they should subscribe to you/pay for your product within seconds. Too often I have found this information buried on a subsidiary page of a website.

When it comes to video, first impressions should be snappy and to the point. If you are employing a high-end ad agency or a top quality copywriter then they will have the experience and ability to tell the story of your product in such a snappy way: you need to employ the same principles when you are making an explanatory video.

REACTION TIME – THE NEED FOR NOW

A great way of making a splash and using social media to create brand awareness is by making a topical video – but it also brings with it plenty of pitfalls. Making a video that riffs off something that is current in the news can bring you a win in terms of views and approval, but even the simplest of videos needs an open mind, courage, trust, buy-in and collaboration from a large cross-section of people inside and outside any typical corporate team.

The major perils are legal and 'taste' – if you get the tone or content wrong then you may well find yourself with egg on your face – or worse, a lawsuit. You don't want to be the latest company to have created a social media SNAFU, and you certainly don't want to have the embarrassment of paying twice for your mistake by hiring a PR team to try and clean up your mess afterwards.

But the upside can far exceed just an impressive set of viewing figures to present at your next monthly marketing meeting. There are plenty of other wins for savvy companies who can get this new, ultra-reactive marketing right. Not just positive sentiments across a range of social networks as well as an increased number of followers and larger fanbase, but also very real and measurable PR wins: especially mentions in the mainstream media.

The American cookie company Oreos showed a now-famous example of this during the SuperBowl in February 2013, when they seized the moment to create an instant marketing message (albeit in image form as opposed to video). When the lights in the stadium went out for 30 minutes due to a power cut and caused a pause in the game, the Oreos marketing team was on hand to create and distribute some fun images that played along with the situation. The resulting ads, which were instantly picked up by bored fans across the country, became a success on social networks and gained Oreos plenty of positive feedback in the mainstream press, not just the trade dailies.

We have had plenty of experience of this by creating a series of comedy topical videos for various clients. But it takes a remarkable degree of latitude from big companies for this to happen. Not to mention speed: as soon as an event occurs, the company and creative team need to be ready to respond. The overall aim here is to make sure these responses are funny enough to be shared (ie go viral) and to attract more people to visit the site in question.

The process to make each video is complex and requires a lot of decisions to be made very quickly. Usually it goes something like this:

Planning: what seems off-the-cuff and instant usually hides a great degree of planning, with a team that understands what it is trying to achieve and trusts each other. It's also a good idea to look at upcoming events and think about how some associated content generation might work for you (being careful not to stand on any legal toes, of course. Other companies may be paying a lot of money for certain sponsorship rights, and may not look too kindly on upstarts crowding their field and trying to steal their thunder).

Idea: the idea is generated usually by a writer or producer, or sometimes by the client. It then has to be turned into some form of workable script. Note that at its most basic level this requires the writer/producer to be alert to what is going on in the media. This means that someone has to be watching for appropriate events (in our company's case this is done pretty much 24/7).

Approval: usually a twofold approval mechanism. Firstly, the client has to like the idea and believe it will improve the 'brand' message. Then – and possibly most importantly of all – the legal department will need to check out the script for any potential legal problems: notably anything potentially libellous, anything that will be a blatant breach of copyright, and anything that will likely cause a cease-and-desist notice, (or worse, land a legal fee on their desk). The grey area here, as we have discussed elsewhere, is the 'breach of copyright' section. If you want to take a piece of footage that has been shown on the news, or use a section of a song , then legally you are breaching copyright. You don't own either. But in the greater scheme of things, unless you are actually demeaning or libelling anyone, you can get away with it, as long as you are keeping music clips to under 30 seconds (it's strongly advisable to use rights-cleared music, or have access to someone who can provide high-quality bespoke music at a reasonable cost). It has become commonplace to see various news clips shown on various YouTube channels, and as we have discussed elsewhere, 'parody' does bring its fair share of legal benefits. This, of course, strictly applies to internet virals: something that may obliquely be benefitting you or your company. It won't work for a mainstream advert, as for this it is essential to clear all rights.

In terms of content and tone though, it is advisable to steer clear of anything too morbid, and even though you only have a short time to make these videos, you need to think long and hard about creating something that is so 'edgy' it may end up having a negative effect on your brand.

Creation: imagine all the time and effort and people involved in making a final version of a brand video: take this and achieve the same thing in a tenth of the time and for a hundredth of the budget. This will give you a rough idea of the work involved in the 'need for speed' process that is creating topical response videos. You need a snappy editor that 'gets it' and can be available day or night, and a producer/writer who can approve/suggest cuts quickly and without the trappings of a Soho edit house, where time can often be on your side. Private YouTube channels, Dropbox and Skype are all fantastically helpful in getting a project made quickly with multiple contributors working remotely.

Distribution: finally, once the video has been approved by the client and given another legal ok, your video is ready to be distributed. Hopefully the news story you are pastiching will still be in the news (it's very disappointing when you make a topical video only to discover that it is no longer topical!), and ideally your brand will already have enough clout (number of Twitter followers, Facebook fans etc) that it will be seen by an audience willing to share.

Of course this process is assuming that you are making a video that is composed of pre-existing news footage or material that you can grab from somewhere online. If you are planning on creating anything more complex, for example involving a set and actors to create a comedy sketch, you have to really figure out how to keep it simple, especially in terms of expense. Once you start paying for set costs, make-up, costumes etc, then your quick reaction skit can become an all-consuming beast: one which ends up costing far more than initially anticipated. If you look at the best examples on sites such as FunnyOrdie or College Humor, you can easily begin to imagine the planning and costs involved, and why the subject matters of their videos are 'semi-topical' rather than 'topical'.

WHAT HAPPENED WHEN THE BEASTIE BOYS SUED

In late 2013, the US toy company Goldieblox released a viral video which used a parody of the Beastie Boys' track 'Girls' as its music theme. Needless to say, the Beastie Boys pounced, and a very public legal battle ensued.

On the one hand, the toy company claimed that their version was acceptable under 'fair use', and that it was actually a beneficial parody as it was encouraging young girls to get involved in science.

On the other, The Beastie Boys is a notoriously litigious group, whose late founder member Adam Yauch stipulated in his will that no company could ever use his music as part of their advertising.

The case went to court, and in early 2014, The Beastie Boys won their case: a settlement was agreed (apparently a charitable donation was made by Goldieblox) and GoldieBlox was forced to publish an apology on its website (as well as counting the cost of producing and distributing the video in the first place). But did it have a negative impact on their business? This is a grey area. How many people would have been put off buying from them because of this? How many people, outside of anyone interested in this type of copyright issue, would have actually *known* about this?

Another grey area is the case itself. While The Beastie Boys were in the right to take action (from their point of view), Goldieblox obviously had expensive legal advice telling *them* that the case was winnable. So there were two sides to this debate, even in 2014. My guess is that the laws will be pushed and pushed until something does eventually break. Had GoldieBlox won this case then it would have opened floodgates for other companies to do the same, all claiming the hard-to-define 'fair use' defence.

But there's yet another complication: some artists from the 1970s and 80s would actually be glad to have their song parodied in such an ad. And they'd even allow it for free. If the resulting video becomes a viral hit and suddenly their song is back in the public psyche, then their overall career may get an unexpected boost. TV ads may pick them up and tour managers may decide to improve the venues they play.

It's a massively complex area: one of the most complex aspects of making viral videos. And it pays to tread carefully. In this instance, a simple search of legal activities on behalf of The Beastie Boys should have set red lights flashing.

MAKING A DOCUMENTARY

Making a documentary is no longer out of your reach. Although the notion of 'viral' leans more towards short-form video, documentaries have their own special cachet. And thanks to modern technology, a documentary is a very realistic goal. Thanks to their resurgence in popularity (Netflix is crowded with documentaries and I often blog about a great recent find), documentaries are also cool.

A particularly good idea for a documentary is to mark a special occasion in the history of a company: particularly an anniversary, such as a 100th or 50th year celebration. What's especially useful is that any company that has been around for a century or half a century is bound to have a wealth of archive material. You'd be surprised how fascinating such nostalgia can be to current or long-term staffers: there may even be archive film material as well that you can use.

A good documentarian should research all of this in tiny detail and work with the company to find out where the focus of the documentary should be. A few days of interviews, with current and previous staff members, as well as any other interested party, should yield plenty of usable material. The filmmaker should also have low overheads: filming and editing being the main aspects of the job.

All this should be achievable for a reasonable figure: there is no reason why a long form piece like this shouldn't cost in the low five figures. And it can mark out a company as having achieved something different and distinctive: something that staff and board members are bound to love, but one which should cause ripples outside of the company as well.

THE VIDEO SALES LETTER

A hot topic in the world of digital marketing in 2014 and 2015 has been the Video Sales Letter (usually abbreviated to VSL). These are short, snappy sales videos, designed to arouse interest and convert viewers into participants. There's an almost old-fashioned appeal to the manner in which they work, and it's definitely worth being aware of what they are and whether there is a part of your business which could work better by having them.

The construction of a video sales letter is pretty straightforward: it's a text-heavy scripted video in which the viewer sees the text on screen as well as hearing it being read out. That's it. A simple combination of the written word, and those same words being read out loud as they appear on screen. It really is that simple, but a lot of testing has gone into figuring out that this is a very effective method of selling (bear in mind these are video *sales* letters).

Of course, in isolation, the video sales letter may not be that effective. They work best as part of an overall strategy. There are plenty of strategies out there which are worth looking into, but usually they involve a hard sell with the video leading the viewer through a series of attractive choices (by making hard-to-resist offers such as beneficial information, promises of mental or physical development, problem-solving etc) which usually start off as free (a PDF booklet about the specific subject matter for example) until the viewer is led to the company's core offer (a 10 session course costing $999 for example).

One criticism of the VSL is that it may come across as *too* direct, and possibly too heavy-handed. That's why it's worth taking care with the tone of the script. A friendly, direct approach which outlines a problem and how the offer contained in the video is a great solution is often an effective approach. It's also worth considering split-testing any VSL campaign: especially if you are planning to do a huge mass launch. It's worth taking the time to refine and put out the best possible product.

Another criticism of the VSL concerns its shelf life as a format. Once viewers have begun to grow familiar with them and their style, then their power may begin to wear off. If a viewer is overtly aware that he or she is being sold to, then they are likely to put up a barrier.

Nevertheless Video Sales Letters can work effectively as part of an arsenal of videos, and are definitely worth having in your toolbox.

TESTING

If you are planning a multi-region video campaign, it's strongly worth considering testing two (or even more) versions of the video. Even more importantly, it's a good idea to test *how* you are going to sell the video, which is most likely to be the headline you use to make people watch in the first place. This is where the use of a good copywriter will be especially helpful – but make sure that they have experience in the online sphere.

If you have a big enough number of followers on Facebook, for example, you can complete a test by specifying that Versions A and B of the video (and even versions C and D with distinct headlines) play in different parts of the target area – or even to different target markets. You can then measure the success of each before undertaking a full rollout. Of course headline-writing is an ever-changing beast, and users are becoming more familiar with, and less likely to look or share, certain over-familiar styles ('You just won't believe Number 11!', for example), so there is an ongoing need to refine and work on how you sell your video as well as the content within.

IT'S NOT ALWAYS ABOUT VIEWS – OTHER WINS

We've seen how the *number* of views may not always be the best measurement of success. It's certainly the most obvious way of measuring a video's reach, and if you are looking to purely create something viral, then numbers are arguably the best way of assessing traffic and eyes.

But depending on your intention, other key ways of assessing a video's success include *quality* of views, *click-through, increased recall, PR wins* and helping you to become a *market leader.* We've already discussed how the quality of your views might sometimes outweigh numbers: if you are creating a very specific campaign targeted at certain individuals, then having their buy-in and appreciation could be the end result you are looking for. In our interview with Ben Piears, we saw how click-through rates are an essential metric if you are creating something like product videos: you should certainly have measurement tools in place to assess the click-through rate, as well as being able to judge how much of your video the viewers are actually watching. And there are plenty of studies which show a vastly improved recall figure for good content that sits well alongside (or is well-integrated into) brand material.

The immediate measurement of the success of content, in terms of its popularity and shareability, is now a mainstay for the leading online news and information providers. The current norm is to track the social network interest in whatever stories are out there and then jump on that trend to provide more and more information or stories about it. This, the logic goes, will increase traffic and views based on accurate figures of what people are looking at and sharing. As a result, many of these organisations tend to push out vast amounts of content with the assumption that only certain stories or videos will succeed: and once success arrives, they then follow up with much more information on that subject. This could be seen as a perfect way of creating content that users actually want, but it also has the possible drawback of losing some potentially valuable content into the internet hinterland. Yet, in my experience, if something is good enough and is pushed out widely enough, it will *usually* find some sort of audience, and if that audience is in turn connected enough, then its natural progression up the social network ladder can begin.

What this means for companies in terms of 'wins' is that they should not despair if success does not come immediately – if a video or other piece of content really has value then it needs that right combination of connections/luck/timing in order to find its place. You don't always have to jump on the latest trend – so much so that if your content is good enough, you can help to *create* the latest trend. And it also means that while measuring the immediate impact of your product is important, an initial underwhelming reaction may not mean the end of your video's potential.

If you operate in a niche area (and as we have seen, nearly all areas are niche – it's just that some niches are bigger than others) then we have seen how creating bespoke content about your field can turn you into a respected voice in your community. And don't underestimate the value of PR: if you manage to make content that is so striking and original that it is picked up by blogs in your particular area, as well as traditional media (newspapers and TV) then you have created something very valuable.

A very good example of how a niche subject matter can combine to provide absorbing video is the YouTube channel for the CrossRail project in London. Crossrail is a huge, multi-billion pound development, which will bring a massive new underground train infrastructure to London by 2018. The work going on under the feet of many Londoners is the biggest project of its kind in Britain since the Channel Tunnel was constructed in the late 80s and early 90s. And CrossRail's Youtube channel is showing the whole process in fabulously interesting detail – the sheer scale of the project, the machines used, the manpower involved are all highlighted in an ongoing series of informative and short videos, which themselves usually achieve a not unimpressive viewing audience in the low five figures.

So remember that it's not *always* about views.

KNOWLEDGE-BASED MEDIA

In the United Kingdom a few years ago there was a popular service by which people could text a question – any question - to a mobile number, and receive an answer in a very short period of time. This service probably still exists, but has been superseded by the prevalence of information and the ease by which it is accessed online. Other knowledge-based sites have taken their own angle into combining the hunger for information and the way it can be user-generated: the question-and-answer service Quora is one of the best current examples.

The sea-change in the way that knowledge is pushed out by media (and increasingly non-media) organisations is such a fascinating topic that it deserves further exploration.

In short, every company or organisation can now add to the information age.

Have you ever been involved in a conversation with your friends or family when someone has brought up a curious trivia fact, or where nobody can remember the name of an actor from a certain film or a certain TV series? The modern-day reaction is no longer to rest in uncertainty – in an instant someone will whip out a mobile, Google it, and provide the answer. Sure, Wikipedia – as it is edited by internet users – may make the (very) odd mistake, but it is usually pretty reliable, and its arrival in the internet age will undoubtedly come to be seen as a turning point for the way in which knowledge is accessed and shared.

People are increasingly tuning in to the fact that the wealth of fascinating information out there can provide them with ongoing mental stimulation. They are no longer – usually – being dictated to by one single news source, as aggregator services such as Flipboard become more and more prevalent. Savvy online presences have realised this: the wealth of different stories (which probably, deep down, all relate to the 'human condition' in some shape or form) from around the world has led to a new 'news' mechanism, which may even be leaving the traditional rolling TV news channels behind. This social-led news curation is often happening simply too quickly for traditional media to figure out what to do with it: which in turn means that in terms of 'breaking news', the social platforms are now the go-to places for information. And while this can have a negative effect as well – you only need to think of the incorrect naming of suspects in a highly trafficked mass-shooting story – it does mean that the knowledge mechanism is rapidly changing ownership, from the traditional media organisations into the hands of those who are capable enough of melding user-led news and old-fashioned reporting.

So where does this leave your organisation and your proposed video content? It means that your product is now part of a much bigger, deeper conversation. In as much as Wikipedia paved the way for the explosion in the new information age from a text point of view, YouTube did exactly the same for video: so much so that anybody who discovers an interest in a new topic will now absolutely expect there to be some relevant video on the subject.

So, if you have something to say about a specific topic, why isn't it *your* video they are watching?

USING MEMBERS OF STAFF IN YOUR VIDEO

I've had the following enquiry several times: 'We'd really like to do something different in our video as we are a bit crazy, you know? A bit wacky. Can we have a video where we are all doing silly things?'

I've gone along with this notion (despite the queasy feeling it usually gives me), turned up, rehearsed people, written some ideas and then a script, made them feel as comfortable as possible and returned to film. And guess what? In front of a camera even the most extrovert sales manager is likely to freeze. And the camera won't lie. It will pick up and even exaggerate any nervous tic or rabbit in the headlights moment and capture it for eternity. So if Joe from sales is the life and soul of the party and is up for doing whatever on camera, think very carefully if he is exactly what you want to show.

Showing a company full of crazy staff might make you stand out in a crowded market place. It might make you memorable. But it might also be embarrassing and end up as a case study of what not to do. Is there any such thing as bad publicity? In this case, maybe. Just as it's necessary to think twice before letting the CEO speak on camera, think equally hard about letting your staff run amok.

DO-IT-YOURSELF: THE PROS AND CONS

The perils of making your own video are numerous: bad lighting, composition, and sound are the chief giveaways. You can always tell. But there can be a place for a no-budget self-made video – on a blog or newsletter for example. But if you are going to take it upon yourself to make your own videos, then consider enrolling in a short class, or, cheaper still, look up some free online lessons in how to frame and light (you might be surprised as to how a basic Anglepoise light can serve a variety of functions).

As long as viewers recognise that you have made an effort, and more importantly that the content is good and relevant, they will forgive a lot of production blips. The other advantage of creating your own content is that you can react quickly to any given situation in your industry - particularly if you are trying to create a blog presence, as well as being able to start your own video library.

I have had clients in the past who have told me that they are considering hiring students to make their films. My standard reply to them is to ask if they would let a student run their business – the quality of the final product as well as the professional experience will always tell in the end.

CUSTOMER TESTIMONIALS/CASE STUDIES

People trust people who are like themselves: who share similar tastes and so on. And the explosion in customer testimonials on web pages underlines how important this is from a sales point-of-view. There has been a gradual move to video in terms of creating customer testimonials, but it is still a space that has plenty of room for expansion. Far too many websites with customer testimonials still have them in written form – which is fine, but it has its limitations, the most obvious being that pages and pages of close text about a certain subject can be off-putting to the reader.

Video testimonials, on the other hand, add life to the review and can often show your product or service being used in a real-life situation by a real member of the public. What's more, they can be inexpensive, as the quality of video does not need to be incredibly high (and there is a certain amount of plausibility in seeing a lo-fi customer review video). It's also something that customers themselves can be persuaded to do at home, for free. If you have a crew of loyal fans who may be interested in your product then it's something that you could easily schedule in to a new release. The popularity of 'unboxing' videos, for the latest piece of digital kit for example, shows just how important a market this has become. So if you regularly launch a new line, or extensions to a current line, then you should definitely consider having your team of customer reviewers ready and waiting.

An extra aspect of this to consider is third party testimonials by journalists and experts in your field. Consumers regard these as extremely useful and reliable if they are deciding to purchase a new product, so why not consider a mix of customer and 'trusted sources'? You do need to be careful in making sure that these people are not over-eulogising your product or service however.

If people suspect that any fakery is involved (for example if the people giving testimony seem like they are acting or following a script) then trust will be quickly lost. It's worth giving some balance to the expert testimonials.

This is an increasingly important area in online video, and striking the right tone and balance is essential: to reiterate, if prospective customers have a whiff that supposedly impartial contributors have been paid or are faking it, they may not stick around too long on your site.

USING YOUR ARCHIVE

In discussing the reasons to consider making a documentary about your company, I mentioned how companies can benefit from using their archive material. What might seem insignificant and dusty might yield a fascinating story which would appeal to a modern audience.

Obviously old footage of a company can be well worthwhile using: current staff members find earlier production techniques both amusing and often eye-opening. Old promotional material can also chart how a company previously promoted itself, and can work well if any contemporary members of staff are able to further expand on their significance, or give interesting accounts of how they were produced. Even a dry old legal document, which may have at one stage had an important role in the life of a company (a sales agreement, or a deal with another company) can be the basis of a tale worth telling.

Humour is another way to breathe life into old footage. We had experience of this when we worked with the writer and presenter David Quantick on a series called 'Making History' for Yahoo Screen. We had the good fortune to be given access to the whole of the Pathe Archive and made 20 comedic episodes looking at aspects of modern life with a nostalgic tint. The series proved popular and the concept was then picked up by other commercial entities who wanted a humorous historical look at their own industries.

Nostalgia has been one of the biggest trends in viral video in the last few years or so. As more and more old footage comes online, people are delighted to see 'the way we were'. If it somehow relates to their current life all the better: a good example in 2014 and 2015 was a 'rare' clip of London in 1927, which showed the city's day-to-day transport situation as a much more serene affair. The modern audience, more accustomed to the stresses of a packed Underground, lapped it up.

Another thing to bear in mind about archive material is that if you don't have any, plenty still exists that you can use. The internet is crammed with public domain footage of the old days, and pretty much all walks of life are covered. We've enjoyed working with companies using this footage to create something relevant to their world in 2015.

So – consider how you could use your archive, or exploit archive material that is out there waiting to be used.

YOUTUBE AUDIO LIBRARY

One of my favourite new resources of the last couple of years has been the YouTube Audio Library, which offers hundreds of high quality pieces that you can download and use as a backing track for your video. There are other similar services, as well as services which offer excellent tracks for a low fee (Audio Networks is very popular in a lot of production offices).

YouTube has entered this space with an impressive offering: not just the amount of tracks (which seems to be increasing), but a pleasing search facility (genre/mood/instrument/duration etc). You can download as many as you like (as long as you re signed in), and from what I can see there are no restrictions on use. Some tracks do ask for a credit, but that is a small price to pay. There are even some well-known classical and seasonal pieces. The only drawback to the service – and one I have never been able to figure out – is the inability to fast forward or jump to a certain part of a track while you are listening to it in the native player. This is a common feature of most audio sites, but YouTube haven't implemented it.

SHOULD YOU ANNOTATE YOUR VIDEOS?

If you've spent any time at all watching YouTube videos, then you'll undoubtedly have seen 'annotated' videos. These are videos that have text overlaid on screen, imploring you to 'click here' in order to find out more information or watch another video. Some marketers are very keen on annotating videos: they see it as akin to banner advertising and something which will increase audience involvement.

If you are thinking about using annotations, then use them wisely. Videos that bombard viewers with annotations can quickly become a turn off. Just because the service exists, it doesn't mean you have to go to extremes in using it. A good piece of advice is to use them just at the beginning and at the end of videos. Successful annotations can indeed lead viewers to a new video of your choice, and if you set them up correctly, they can even take viewers to your own website to purchase or sign up.

WHAT IS YOUR COMPETITOR DOING?

You should know not only who your competition is, what their sales are, how they market, but also how they are representing themselves socially and visually. If they are producing virals that are gaining hundreds of thousands or even millions of views, then you may need to act and make some of your own. But don't forget that you can employ social scoring to see what people are saying about your competitors as well, from their latest product releases to their latest videos.

INTERVIEW – ANDREA MANN

Andrea Mann is the former comedy producer at Huffington Post UK and is now a freelance writer and broadcaster. (Full disclosure: we've worked with Andrea on creating a number of Topical video virals for AOL/Huffington Post UK, and this interview was done while she was still in the role.)

Q: Is it possible to 'know' that a video will go viral?

AM: Sometimes it really is. An example from 2014 I can think of was that of a fat man dancing by a hotel pool along to some aerobics music, and as soon as I saw it I knew people would love it. The element of surprise is important, but I think joyousness and silliness is a big thing. You also know in terms of the coverage that it's getting.

Q: How do you find videos before they have gone viral?

AM: 99% of the time I don't find the video on YouTube. I find it because I look every single morning at about 8 websites, such as Viral Viral videos, Most Watched Today, Daily Picks and Flicks, and Laughing Squid. Tastefully Offensive is very good at picking good videos, helping to make them go viral, and they never put any comments around them - they literally just post up the video. So if I come in in the morning, and I see the same video on three of those websites then I know that it's already started to go viral. Otherwise it's kind of instinct because you might see the video just on one of those websites and immediately think - this will go viral. Literally every morning when I sit at my desk I have 20 windows set up to open automatically so I don't miss anything.

PH: Andrea mentions the key word of joy here, as well as silliness and the element of surprise. Snarky, pointed videos do have their place and can reach a lot of viewers, but in general, videos that make viewers happy have a better chance at succeeding. It's also important to underline the chain that exists in making videos go big – whether it's being featured on one of the sites mentioned above or being powered through the Twitter ecosystem or similar. But note that the role YouTube plays in the initial 'finding' – YouTube tends to come into play later on, as a repository for successful videos.

Q: So YouTube is not your main or even your first source for finding these videos?

AM: No. I want to find that funny video of a man dancing by a pool when its got 200 views, because the fewer places that have covered it the more likely it is that you're going to be a source for someone to see it. The man dancing was a classic example: I found it late that afternoon, I put it live when it had just a few hundred views on YouTube. The only place I'd seen it at that point was on Totally Offensive. Lo and behold the next morning there were thousands of Facebook likes on the post that I had made, and people were really talking about it.

But people still think of YouTube as the first source for watching that funny video that everyone's talking about. It doesn't matter whether I put the URL to my link on Huffington Post, you'll see that a lot of people then just take the YouTube link. But they then click on the video within your post to find the original, there's still a 'purity' to it. I think also when you just post a YouTube link on Twitter and Facebook it looks cooler - it looks like you found it. I can see why people go for YouTube. The fact that you can play YouTube videos and other types of videos in Facebook is very important to their success, I think.

PH: What's interesting is this relationship between the main players. YouTube may not always be the first place people will find videos, but once it has had success they will expect it to appear on YouTube.

It's key that your video is immediately playable on every network. Always check how the link works on Twitter and elsewhere (Twitter has made a lot of progress with native and embedded video but a lot of the time people still have to click away to view). And always make sure you check how the video will play on a mobile phone – I have seen plenty of good videos ruined by simple mistakes, such as having a font that is simply too small to read on a mobile.

Q: How do you see the differences between Facebook and Twitter in terms of sharing video?

AM: I still think of Twitter as being really a place where people share information and opinions, first and foremost, as opposed to sharing videos, and maybe that's because it still usually requires that extra click. I think Facebook is really important and that's where it really gains traction, because it is probably the place where you know far more people who are actually using the social network. Facebook's more 'normal', for want of a better word. I think the average person in the street is on Facebook, they're not necessarily on Twitter and they're not all talking about politics. But then again we have more Twitter followers than we have Facebook likes and we can use lots of different accounts.

PH I have obviously talked a lot about the importance of Twitter in boosting a video's views but there is a basic message here: not everyone is on Twitter. And if they are not on it by now, it might be on its way to reaching saturation point. This certainly seems the case in early 2015, with many social media commentators discussing the stagnation or even possible demise of Twitter's audience. Twitter may certainly seem more 'instant' than Facebook, but in the longer term it is key to have success on Facebook as well. If you have a lot of likes and shares on Facebook, then you know you are on to a good thing.

Q: When is the best time to send out a video for maximum effect?

The best days for video are Monday to Thursday. Weekends are always quieter - traffic is always quieter then. This will probably have skewed since the popularity of Facebook because basically most people use the computer when they're at work. They're on Facebook, they're on Twitter or they're on websites looking at YouTube and cat videos when they should be working. Facebook has more traffic apparently in the evenings than at weekends. So the whole 'When do people use the internet?' question has skewed slightly. What has also skewed it is the Tweeting along and the reactions to TV programmes. You get some of that on Facebook but it always seems to be after the event - it's always more 'Did anybody see this tonight?' It's not as live as Twitter. Facebook is more evenings than weekends, while Twitter is during the day. You'll have a burst of Facebook at mornings and lunchtimes…
We tweet things about 3 times - we push out a story a few times, maybe with different wording every time from different accounts. But you have to be careful - you don't want to overdo it so you're annoying everyone by sending out the same old Tweets.

PH: Quite often I have seen examples where businesses make a video, send it out once and nothing happens. And then they leave it and consider it all a big failure. This is from usually companies who have the 'let's make a viral!' mentality – the thinking that just making the video automatically leads to success. But it's essential not to stop at the first hurdle. The reality is much more complex – if the video is not part of an overall marketing strategy then it will definitely end in disaster. And if it's not sent out at the right time, or multiple times, to the right people, then you are diminishing your chances of success to an even greater degree.

Q: Should corporations be jumping on trends in virals and making their own 'in-house' versions of comedy virals?

AM: I'm not sure they're doing that so much these days. I've seen obviously the Harlem Shake they did on a few American TV shows. (PH The 'Harlem Shake' phenomenon hit its peak in 2013 – countless organisations and institutions were doing their own version of this viral video). I think what companies try to do instead is make a video that's 'going to go viral'. I think that's the heart of it really, rather than jumping on bandwagons. But I see them so obviously and deliberately doing this: there's a lot of arrogance.

PH There is a lot of arrogance but there is also a lot of ignorance. The mantra of 'let's make a viral video!' is still surprisingly used quite commonly by many companies I encounter. But as Andrea clearly points out – you are making a video in the hope that it will go viral.

Q: Is there a sense that the market for these kinds of videos is overcrowded?

AM: It's very crowded: I don't know how you define overcrowded. I think as long as there are good videos out there and anyone can make what they want and put it up, I don't think it's a bad thing that the place is getting overcrowded but I do think it means that you have to be really good to get your stuff noticed.

It just always boils down to whether it's good enough or not. So many pranks have been done for example - they've always been done since the day of Candid Camera. People will always like prank videos and prank videos often will go viral of course, but I think it has to be something quite nice and sweet.

PH Some key things to take away here. Your content needs to stand out, be unique and attention-grabbing to catch people's time. And once again we see how joy is often a better approach than snarkiness. Often companies need to give themselves a reality check about what it is that they have actually produced – if everyone has drunk the Kool-Aid and PR companies are being paid to push the video then they are frequently lulling themselves into a false sense of security and self-belief that in no way responds to real world reactions about their product. And finally, don't ignore the basics.

Q: So quality is key? Don't celebrities always bring a guaranteed audience?

AM: It's all about the product, the quality of the writing and the quality of the production. People think if you attach a star name to it, it will be a success, but not if it's a bad script, and not if it's not really well done. If it's a bit like the Wayne Rooney Skyfall video where I think we kind of knew instinctively that that was really good: if something is really good it will probably fly. It's not that you deliberately try and make one good and one not so good, or you try to make one go viral and the other one not go viral: you just try and make it as good as possible.

PH: The Wayne Rooney video was one of ours, and one that we worked on with Andrea for The Huffington Post. We created it in the run-up to the release of the James Bond 'Skyfall' film, with the bizarre but amusing concept of having the footballer Wayne Rooney playing James Bond. The video became a big success upon release, ending up with a large number of views and getting plenty of reblogging and coverage in the newspapers. It was even discussed on an Argentine breakfast TV show. This was also a very good example of an 'extra' win – going beyond just the number of views, as all of the third party coverage mentioned us as the original source.

'Quality' can be a rather arbitrary and subjective thing. It's become a common enough mantra that 'lo-fi' is fine for online video, that viewers will accept hastily or poorly made videos since it's the 'idea' that is all-important. But as the internet age progresses, this is increasingly not true: jolts and errors in a video will, ultimately, detract from its success. Production standards have risen tremendously in the last couple of years, even when it comes to using existing material which may have glitches (that's why, when creating a video from existing footage it's always better to find the best quality that you possibly can), and certainly also in terms of onscreen graphics, which can enhance a video and take it to the next level.

Q: Have all the ideas been done?

AM: You think there are no new ideas left under the sun and then someone will come up with something really brilliantly done and it reinvents the genre it or it gives you a whole new lease of life. It could be down to the choreography of a particular flashmob, or the song that they used was particularly great.

PH I think it might have been John Lennon who posited that pop music was on the way out because all of the available notes had been used in all their possible orders. Lennon wasn't quite right, as time has shown, and while new and different genres of music still pop up, it's something that is relatable to video content. While certain style of videos do persist (flashmobs being one - the Harlem Shake videos were a subset of the *flashmob), it's still eminently possible to be innovative. And particularly given that the barrier to entry is so open now, it literally just requires a great idea to be well-executed.*

Q: And how important is joy in all of this?

AM: It's coming up with the right idea at the right time and just executing it really well. I don't think it matters whether it's one person on their own with a camera doing it from their bedroom or it's a company spending millions of pounds on it. It's all in the writing and the execution. You can give pranks a whole new lease of life. There are some Bad Lip Reading ones that are better than others, and there are some Honest Movie Trailers that are better than others. But sometimes there are really simple ideas: for example recently there was a video of Laurel and Hardy dancing to the Rolling Stones. It was just so simple and so joyous.

These little slices of joy - that's the thing. Obviouslt, there is always going to be obviously schadenfreude, but it's part of human nature to enjoy brilliance. That's why you want to go and see an Oscar-winning performance or a wonderful West End show that people love, or great bands playing live. I think that's just a really human thing. So if a video in and of itself gives you that special little feeling of joy....

PH: I love Andrea's expression 'little slices of joy'. It defines perfectly what a lot of online videos should be aiming for.

POST-VIDEO ANALYSIS: 8 MORE THINGS

There are many ways in which you can assess the success or failure of a video campaign. If infiltration into mainstream media and millions of views is the upper benchmark, there are plenty of other things you should be looking out for, including:

1. Track where your views are coming from. Has a potential new market for your service or product appeared as a result of your video?

2. Similarly, track the engagement on the video across all the social networks. Who is talking about it? Are they existing or potentially new customers? And are the prospective new customers talking about your video in a different way to your existing followers? It's simple to do this on Twitter and you should do it with every video you release to the public as a matter of course. Needless to say, if you have lost longtime followers because of a video then you will need to understand why.

3. Check the peaks and troughs of the online reaction to your video. Create a timeline which corresponds with when you released the video and any subsequent pushes you may have done. Assess whether the video has a short shelf life or not: if it doesn't then you may consider re-releasing it at a future time.

4. You should work out the 'potential reach' of your video as well as the actual number of views counted. This is not just the number of people who have mentioned you or retweeted you, but their total audience as well. There are plenty of tools and services to help you do this.

5. Are people referring you? Is there a call-to-action included in your proposition, such as an easy link for them to use to recommend you?

6. If you do have a call-to-action, how successful has it been?

7. Have you had a spike in one channel over any of the others you use? For example, have your Vine videos done significantly better than your Instagram or YouTube ones? If so, it may be that your service or manner of promoting it is particularly suited to that channel, and it may be one to concentrate further resources on.

8. Did the campaign meet, surpass, or fail to live up to, your expectations? If you wanted to engage more followers, did that happen? If you had a specific call-to-action, did it work? This is a pretty basic necessity of any video post-mortem.

INFLUENCERS: NON-CELEBRITIES

We've seen how celebrities are an increasingly weak overall group to rely upon for getting the word out about your video. They certainly still *can* have an effect, but because it's just so hard to get their attention due to the sheer numbers of social media requests they have, and because of other corporate demands on their time/sponsorship value, it's very rare that a celebrity will actually 'break' your film to a wider audience.

So who should you be focussing on in terms of helping you to get the video out there?

In short, advocates/superfans/influencers in your field. If you have a decent social media presence then you can easily identify who these people are. And with some simple tactics (ie rewarding them for spreading the word), you will find that they will probably be more than happy to do so. Of course, this field of influence can also apply to figures of authority in your field: the more 'official' voices you have giving the thumbs up to a film you have made, the better.

DON'T WORRY IF IT DOESN'T ALL MAKE SENSE

If you make a list of what you believe to be the Top 10 most popular TV ads, it's likely that a fair smattering of animated characters, surreal plotlines and things that may not make obvious sense feature among them. And now go back to the pitching process when the agency presented its unusual new idea to the client. What at first may have seemed plain weird or just too 'out there' might have turned into a successful multi-million dollar campaign putting the product or service into the national consciousness.

The same logic can apply to video virals. Not everything has to make complete sense. Sure, you can back up your ideas with as many statistics and projections as you'd like, but it's good to occasionally take a leap of faith on something that may simply seem instinctively successful.

This particularly applies to comedy virals. Not every single aspect of each video has to make sense. This can often create internal battles before the video is released ('That would never happen'), but audiences are much more willing to see something unusual than many small to medium businesses might think. Compared to adverts, virals are much less expensive, so there are many more opportunities to be creative.

IDEAS CAN COME FROM ANYWHERE

Iconoclastic thought, or thinking differently and in a new way about something, is a really useful tool to develop when working on viral videos (it's useful for all creative thinking). There are ways and means of working on iconoclastic thought, but an important way in which you can create something that stands out is never to dismiss, even if an idea seems random or tangential.

Random ideas can come from anywhere. Conversation is a good place to generate them, and this is what happened when we developed our 'Tory Supermarket' viral video in early 2015, a video that went on to be widely shared.

THE POWER OF MUSIC

Don't underestimate the importance of the music you choose for your video. Many ordinary videos have been greatly enlivened by a judicious choice of music – and equally, any music or sound that is particularly annoying (or passé) can work against you. Music is a very subjective thing, so it can take time to find the right track. In our interview, Andrea Mann indicated that she might have a preference for finding a new piece of music through a video or an ad, so bear in mind that it doesn't always have to be a well-known track (which will often be out of your price range anyway in terms of licensing costs).

If you are creating something for a small, one-off private event, then you are usually going to get away with using any track or tracks you like, but if it's anything that is going to be shown in the public arena, then make sure that you have looked carefully at the rights implications: it's not nice to receive a takedown notice after the event. If you are looking for a low-cost alternative, then there are plenty of excellent off-the-shelf services which will offer you a selection of very high quality music at reasonable prices. These can become overused though, so again ensure that the track you are using isn't one that is heard every day.

Of course, as we have seen with Psy, it is possible to use a brand new track that is a hit if the conditions are right: ideally if you are spoofing something, paying homage to something or doing something that will enhance the popularity of the track itself, then the rights-holders may take a more lenient approach. This was the case when we worked on a video for the Daft Punk mega-hit 'Get Lucky'.

BRINGING THE JOY WITH DAFT PUNK

One of our own examples of what we can call 'bringing the joy' was a video we made with David Schneider for The Huffington Post in the spring of 2013, for the new Daft Punk track 'Get Lucky'. At the time the track was a global phenomenon: a hugely anticipated single from the mysterious French electronic duo, that meshed their unique sensibilities with a late 70s and early 80s disco vibe (thanks in no small part to the participation of Chic's Nile Rodgers). It was nigh on impossible in May and June of 2013 to spend too long listening to the radio without hearing 'Get Lucky'.

One of the most important aspects of the release of the single was that the band didn't initially provide a video. This meant several things for aspiring content producers around the world. Rather like the manner in which Psy released 'Gangnam Style' twelve months earlier to remixers and open sourcers, the Daft Punk phenomenon gave anyone who had an idea and the wherewithal to make a video free rein. And there were several really good efforts: the English comedian Peter Serafinowicz made a typically out-there video in which he played a three-headed character singing along and dancing to the track. Someone else had the inspired idea of showing Celine Dion, in her full Vegas regalia, funking out to the track. These, and many others, captured millions of views between them. They also gave Daft Punk a worldwide platform: their song was now so 'cool' that the best video remixers were making versions to accompany it.

Our own effort stemmed from a simple idea: what if everyone from the movies danced to 'Get Lucky'? Travolta from Saturday Night Fever (and several other Travolta films), Jamie Bell from Billy Elliot, Gene Kelly, Jennifer Beals and even Eric Idle from a

Monty Python dance sequence. The result – expertly edited by Lisa Marsh – definitely had the elusive joy factor. It's probably something about dancing per se, and especially dance sequences from classic films, but it definitely hit a chord and was soon being spread around the world. We had taken 2 or 3 seconds maximum from each film, synched them up with the track, and made 4 minutes of sheer happiness. It was blogged about, reblogged, featured in several online newspapers and was picked up by many of the celebrities who featured in it: Jamie Bell, Jennifer Grey and even Ricky Gervais all retweeted it (Gervais alone has over 5 million Twitter followers), showing that - given the right circumstances – celebrities will still retweet something to give it greater exposure.

The lesson of our Daft Punk experience isn't complex or deep: on the contrary it taps into a simple primitive human need to have a good time. The song already lent itself to that: our video, hopefully, captured its spirit and showed that – generally speaking – smiles usually beat snarks.

THE JOY OF HORROR

It was October 2013. A viral video based on one of the scariest
horror films had achieved 10 million views. *In two days.*

How was this – in any way – joyful?

The backstory begins with the success of the 1970s book 'Carrie'
by Stephen King, about a young girl who is ostracised at school
for her perceived 'strange' ways, and wreaks revenge using her
telekinetic powers. Such was the success of the original film
version, dreamily directed by Brian di Palma, that the film became
a staple watch during the early years of the home video boom. It
became embedded in a certain section of the western psyche – and
showed that just as people love to laugh and share joy, they love
to be scared and share frights as well. Carrie, like The Omen or
The Exorcist, tapped into a new horror in the 1970s, and changed
the genre.

So when MGM decided to remake the film for a 2013 audience,
and thought about how to promote it, they tapped into this deeper
knowledge of the Carrie trope that is shared amongst older
viewers, and created an advertising viral that attracted their key
target audience – teens – in their millions. So much so that the key
question in terms of video virals in October 2013 was 'have you
seen the Carrie video'?

MGM hired Thinkmodo, a US-based video company who
specialise in creating stunt videos that attract a *lot* of attention.
The company employed a Candid Camera-style technique to
convince diners in a café that they were in the presence of a girl
with telekinetic powers. That was the gist – viewers were in on the
joke and were fascinated by the reaction of the diners in the café,

who really believed, even for a split second, that they were witnessing a life-changing event.

There was lots of ensuing press about just how much of the video was real or fake (were the customers in the café actors?) but this is beside the point. As well as a traditional media campaign to promote the film, MGM had reams of coverage across the social networks, a hugely increased recognition rate for their film, and a surefire box office winner: or was it? Despite having little competition in the traditionally busy Halloween horror spot, Carrie debuted to a relatively disappointing opening weekend of $17 million: a third place in the charts. Which goes to show that even the best and most successful video viral will *still* need to be part of a good overall campaign, and if the final product isn't up to scratch then success will be even more difficult (Carrie received middling reviews at best).

One explanation for the subsequent box office failure of the film is that while fear is hugely effective as a way of focussing the mind and the emotions, it doesn't have a huge influence on the purchase or decision-making ability. It concentrates people so intensely that their desire to act on it is diminished. So, with videos that are intended to make people acquire something based on fear, it's wise to tread carefully. One of the techniques commonly used in the Video Sales Letters, which we have discussed elsewhere, is to play upon a customer's fear. If they didn't have a specific product or service, for example, how much less happy or successful would they be? This is a different type of fear than the horror example above, which is all about persuading people to pay to have a scary experience. If you can portray yourself as some sort of shield to prevent your customer experiencing something they are afraid of, it could well be worth exploring.

EMBRACE THE PARODIES OF YOUR WORK

There's a huge chain of retailers in Britain called John Lewis who produce a much-loved annual television ad. It's an 'event' moment – akin to the SuperBowl ads every January. Every year, they release their ad to the internet early one Friday morning in November. By the afternoon, the spoofs begin to hit the net. There are so many satirists who have access to editing facilities that spoofs hit the web hours after the event.

Embrace this. The huge chain certainly did. All the 2012 spoofs (one of which was ours) were collated and sent to their head office for their next big marketing powwow. The bigwigs loved it. And why shouldn't they? This is, essentially, free marketing. An indication that their brand is so strong and so familiar that people are able to work on its riffs and rhythms immediately.

When we had success with our Chilean miners fake film trailer in 2010, ABC News in the United States put it on the front of their website. They were delighted to be associated with something that was perceived as cool, humorous and zeitgeisty.

Don't think of copyright in the same old way. By all means protect what is yours. But this is very different from the world of music copyright. If you are clever enough to create a viral video, one that stands above the masses and gets noticed, you should take it as an honour that people spoof it.

Embrace it.

BE HUMAN

Whether you are using video, social networking or traditional marketing, never forget that your potential customer is a human. And since the advent of the internet – through forums, message boards, and latterly blogs, Twitter and Facebook, they are humans armed to the teeth with a variety of measures to comment on your activity. If you do something wrong, and particularly, fail to treat your potential customers as humans, they will let you know. Your reputation is everything, so be human in everything you do – this applies to any films you create as much as any other marketing you employ.

THE MOST COMMON VIDEO MISTAKES START-UPS MAKE

1. Throwing everything into the video. Keep it simple!

2. Telling 'their' story, as opposed to explaining simply what the product is and what solution it provides.

3. Not having a big enough budget. Because most start-ups are short on cash and have got where they are thanks to a lot of favours (barter/promises/begs/steals or borrows), they can have an unrealistic idea of how much to spend on a video. They can also have unrealistic expectations of what the video will look like and how it will be made. This can also lead to scope-pushing.

4. Scope-pushing (wanting a $1000 product but only being prepared to spend $100) is very common amongst start-ups, and it's one reason that a lot of video companies refuse to work with them.

5. Not allocating the right person to oversee the project, and not having a correct workflow in place for giving feedback. Start-ups are particularly prone to showing the final version of a video to the boss only at the last minute. If the boss requires major changes, this can prove tricky.

6. Placing too much importance on the video. Start-ups should be prepared to fail in many ways, and they should realise that a video is not the be all and end all. It can (and should) help but if their business isn't fundamentally sound in the first place, no video can turn that around.

7. Not having a distribution strategy. We've discussed this time and time again over the course of the book. It's paramount at any level, especially for a start-up.

8. Not realising the sheer amount of time needed to be devoted to the project. In the maelstrom of actually starting a business from scratch, certain things tend to get overlooked, or not given enough attention. Videos can be one of them. They take one of the most precious resources at this point: time. Make sure you devote enough to it.

9. Falling into the trap of making their video look like every other start-up video. This was especially the case two or three years ago, when it seemed that every new start-up video wanted to ape the style of Apple or Google. As a result, many videos got lost. Push your envelope and think outside of your box. Don't be afraid to take risks – if you want to get noticed then you have to really make some innovative noise to support your new offering.

10. Failing to keep records of who is sharing their material, and commenting on it. This is the start of an essential user database, and apart from the time it takes to put it all together, it's pretty much free! If you're gaining fans and advocates from the get-go then it's crucial to capitalise on that – the 'early adopter' mentality works just as well for fans of new websites as it does for goods and services.

11. Forgetting to have a 'follow me' button or similar. If you're attracting hundreds or thousands of potential new customers who are actively sharing your videos, you need to make sure you keep them in the loop on any further developments or releases. The internet is so vast, so rapidly changing, that people soon forget things that they may have initially appeared extremely keen on. If

you've got their attention early on, then make sure you do your best to keep it.

TESTING

There are some online digital marketing communities where testing is seen as the Holy Grail. According to this mantra, everything should be tested ad infinitum: the message, the thumbnail, the first five seconds, the headline, the call-to-action...

One of the unspoken problems with this attitude is that so much time can be taken up, and so much value put on testing that the bigger picture starts to be ignored. People can spend an inordinate amount of time and place so much weight on testing that they become stuck in 'test' mode. Just as some start-ups get stuck in 'planning' mode, the importance of numbers can, from time to time, be overemphasised. This can affect the ability of a campaign to move dramatically and to react as necessary. And the figures may not always tell the truth.

One area that it is important to test however is the call-to-action. This usually appears at the end of the video and encourages the viewer to do something: to purchase, to find out more, or to view more videos. It's key to get the language of the call-to-action just right, and it is one area where it is worth spending time to do some split testing to find out which set of words works best for you. If you have access to a good copywriter, now is the time for him or her to show their mettle, and if not it is worth engaging their services on a part-time basis. A good thing about getting the call-to-action just right for you or your company is that once you have cracked your particular code, you may not need to worry about trying to recreate the wheel again and again: if you find a call-to-action that works for you, then users will ideally become familiar with it and you can use it again and again.

FOCUS ON THE ONE THING

Do you ever watch an ad on TV and wonder why it seems so tacky? And it just repeats the same message again and again? There's a pretty basic advertising maxim that simple repetition of one message is the way to introduce a new concept or item for sale to members of the public. And this same idea needs to flow into your corporate video. This is *especially* true if you are a start-up. You might have a funky new name and a funky new idea. Initially, in your video and film choices, you should just be thinking about explaining who you are and what you do in as simple a manner as possible. I have talked to start-up companies far too often who want to talk about the *ten* benefits their product can bring. It's easy, and understandable to be excited about your new product, but if you have hired someone to create ideas and films for you then let them do their job. Simplicity, and an outsider's perspective, will more often than not be far more valuable than shoehorning-in multiple messages.

A FUN WAY OF FIGURING OUT IF YOUR CONTENT HAS 'MADE IT'

There are plenty of scientific ways of tracking how well a piece of content is doing once it is released. But a fun, completely informal and unscientific way of figuring out if your content has made it (ie penetrated the mainstream, or the mainstream of the niche you are operating in) is to pay attention to the main social networks and see if your particular social group has shared it. This could be your friends group on Facebook or one of the people you follow on Twitter. It shows that you must be doing something right: if your friends retweet or share a piece of content *without* knowing that you were involved in its creation, it's far more satisfying than a 'pity' favourite or a forced share. It's also, obviously enough, a nice boost to your professional ego.

WHAT ARE YOU DOING FOR THE NEXT THIRTY SECONDS OF YOUR LIFE?

It's common to see an article talking about the new era of shortened attention spans. But this isn't really true at all. People are still devouring content of the same traditional length. They are still watching films and reading books in their millions. Except these days, it's just as likely to be on a VOD service like NetFlix or a electronic reader like the Kindle as it is the cinema or a physical book you can hold in your hand.

What has changed – and there is increasingly no dispute about it – is the life cycle of content. It's common now to read about the '24 hour life cycle' of a news story. This is *almost* true: while some news stories last for days or weeks, a lot of them fade into recent history fairly quickly. But where the life cycle has really diminished is the life cycle of general viral content. Popular stories, comedy videos, viral phenomenon are increasingly going very big very quickly and then disappearing into memory. The next story or viral is just a click or a share away.

It's another reason why, when creating content, it's increasingly important to focus on content with legs – that is, content which has some potential for an evergreen lifespan. And it's also why it's increasingly hard to win the battle for the next thirty seconds of a viewer's life. There are so many other pieces of content vying for exactly the same attention.

IS EMAIL REALLY DEAD AS A SHARING TOOL?

We discussed earlier how email is sometimes now seen as the preserve of the older generation when it comes to sharing online video. But that's not to say that email is itself dying out. In fact, it is undergoing a resurgence in terms of marketing and the last couple of years have seen a spike in its popularity for online marketers. A key distinction that email has over Facebook and Twitter, and one which is now being harnessed by marketers, is that it is much less time-sensitive. With Twitter and Facebook, a user will generally only see what is relatively recent in his or her timeline as they are unlikely to scroll back too many hours or days to look at older posts. Email doesn't have that problem: it sits in the inbox and can be opened at leisure, and if it comes from a trusted source then its chance of being opened and read is high. Which is another advantage of email: it's much more personal.

One of the first things anyone did when they went online for the first time was to acquire an email address. These addresses are often carried around for years: my own personal address is at least 15 years old. Of course, in the meantime I have obtained several new addresses, mainly in the course of different jobs and roles I have undertaken. I have friends with over 10 email addresses (which can present a challenge when it comes to picking the right one from my address list). People have a personal address, and multiple work ones. Some people feed all their emails, from the multiple addresses, into one place. Others, like me, regard each email address as serving a different purpose. It's almost as if they enter a different state of mind when they look at each email address: from the more 'personal' to the more 'professional'.

For a while many experts proclaimed email was dead. It was too cumbersome. It was ineffective. It was sucking attention in the workplace and diverting people away from doing their actual job. Pretenders to the email throne came and went. Google Wave was one such example: a new 'communications platform', it was meant to supersede email and provide us with a more efficient way of communicating. It didn't take off and was quietly put to rest in 2012. Project management tools also emerged to take some of the heat off email: running huge projects with hundreds of people, all via email, was simply a very inefficient way of doing things. That's why tools such as Basecamp, Podio, Box (and a myriad of others) became hot properties and essential applications for larger projects. On an individual basis, the rise of notetaking and personal planning apps also took some of the functionality away from emails. Shareable, simple apps such as Evernote and Wunderlist have allowed people to run their days more efficiently.

But – and it's a big but – email has survived. Quite possibly because it's a very personal thing to most people. And it allows them to communicate personally with whoever they are writing. This is why the rise of the email marketing list and the daily email has become such a hot topic for marketers in the last couple of years. If you have 10,000 people interested in your product, and more especially what you have to say about it, and if you are prepared to write a daily, informal email to them about the subject, something they will look forward to receiving at a certain time and which feels personal to them, then you have a very valuable commodity.

Now, imagine you have this list, this receptive and happy audience who actually look forward to receiving your emails (this is way beyond traditional blurb or bland mass-marketing messages), and you decide to insert some links or videos into these emails. The click-through rates are *hugely* impressive, with some email marketers claiming open rates of over 20%. It's person-to-person communication from a trusted source, so people are more likely to follow the link. I know I do: I have at least three daily emails that I look forward to receiving. They are from people, not organisations. Of course they are trying to sell me something, but it's an honest exchange: there's no hard sell here. And if they miss out a day I begin to wonder if the writers are ok. This isn't random, occasional emailing. This is *seven days a week*. It's not even annoying: I could choose to leave the email service any day I wanted. And I'm not saying I am buying a huge amount from these people but one thing is for certain: I know who they are, they entertain me, they educate me about an area I am actively interested in, and when the time comes for me to make a purchase in their field (or recommend someone to do so), they are probably going to be the first person I will turn to.

SOME YOUTUBE FACTS AND STATS

1. In June 2014, there were just under *11 billion* video views on YouTube. In November 2015, this had increased to *8 billion per day*. You can guess what this figure will be in June 2016.

2. According to a 2014 Levels Beyond survey, 67% of people are actively interested in how to/instructional brand sponsored videos – if the content is compelling enough – and 42% of viewers want to watch funny material from brands. Yet, astonishingly, 75% of marketers are not using video on a regular basis to get this across.

3. The time it takes to reach one billion views on YouTube is getting shorter and shorter. Psy was the first to do it with 'Gangnam Style' in 2012. In 2015, Wiz Khalifa and Charlie Puth did it in under six months with 'See You Again'. In early 2016, it took Adele 3 months to do it with 'Hello'.

4. Popular YouTube videos are increasingly being ripped from the site and posted as native Facebook videos. Often, the person ripping them will remove any original branding or logos. It's worth bearing in mind and keeping an eye on if you have a hit video and it suddenly appears on Facebook.

5. Less than 10% of small businesses in the US use YouTube to host their videos. Extraordinary but true.

6. 80% of YouTube views come from outside the United States. The world is watching – so give your video a global chance of success.

7. Likewise, 85% of online adults (outside of China) consider themselves 'regular' users of YouTube.

8. The number of channels earning six figures through YouTube is increasing at a rate of 50% year-on-year. YouTube has paid out well over $1 billion in royalties.

IF THREE HOURS IS A LONG TIME IN POLITICS WHAT DOES IT MEAN FOR BUSINESS?

Towards the end of 2014, the former British government adviser Dominic Cummings gave an extraordinary speech to a business conference in which he dished the dirt on his former employers. It wasn't hugely reported but it painted an amazing picture of a government which focussed purely on 'the next few days'. Instead of thinking about long-term goals and how to achieve them, Cummings was reported in The Guardian newspaper as pointing out that one of the British Prime Minister's top advisors spent most of his time 'running around with a ridiculous grid which is worrying about Twitter and the news cycle for the next three hours'.

Cummings described the situation as a farce, and if what he claims is true, it's hard to disagree with him. This isn't a situation that is just the domain of politics however. In my experience it's an affliction that can equally affect business. The lesson that can be taken away for business is clear: yes, it's important to monitor the results of a campaign, especially an online video campaign when the statistics are so easily available to track, but don't let it detract from your core business. Are you still striving to improve your core offering or service on a daily basis? Are you trying to take steps to stand out from the crowd in your marketplace? These, and plenty of other points like them, are the crucial stepping stones of developing a business. Panicking about short-term goals, as in our political example (and they are in the business of running a huge economy), is just going to raise the stress levels and help to create a headless chicken culture. In short, when it comes to social media and video campaigns, try and take a longer term view.

IS IT WORTH TRYING TO MAKE YOUR OWN 'ICE-BUCKET CHALLENGE'?

In the summer and Autumn of 2014 it was impossible to go anywhere on the internet without getting a residual splash from someone doing, or talking about, the Ice Bucket Challenge. It became *the* charity phenomenon of the year, and sent those involved in cause-related social media scuttling to find the follow-up.

The Ice Bucket Challenge was somewhat based on a false premise, though (which actually was part of its brilliance). Most people didn't actually know what they were raising money for (and, in its voyage across the Atlantic, the main recipient of money raised changed identity), but they still did it in their millions. It was what Hollywood marketers would call a four-quadrant phenomenon, appealing to young and old, male and female. It was fun to watch, slightly (but not too) hard to do, and made people feel good about themselves. The 'challenge' aspect fostered a natural sharing element, with people videoing themselves in their millions all over the world. It even had celebrity endorsement (a key driver at the start of the campaign).

So, should companies go all-out to find their own Ice Bucket Challenge in 2016? There are pros and cons. Plenty of other organisations have tried to create their own version, with varying degrees of success: from no make-up selfies to wake-up selfies to UNICEF's Commonwealth Games Opening Ceremony 'moment', when Ewan McGregor implored those watching to text for charity (and helped to raise a very impressive £3m). But most of the ones we have heard of have had the backing of large charities with seasoned social media teams, funds to promote it, and early celebrity endorsement. For every no make-up selfie campaign, there are probably 10 (or more) which didn't even make it above the parapet. Users are also jaded, with a certain amount of charity fatigue and cycnicism also having set in.

That's not to say it's impossible, but it is a complex issue: with correctly managed expectations, diligence and (above all) a unique and shareable concept, it might be worth thinking about. It's also worth considering the long-term ramifications: are you actually creating 'advocates' who will support you, or just short-term 'slactivists' who are more or less fulfilling a box-ticking requirement and won't remember who you are in six months' time? It might actually be a better policy to focus on creating longer-term awareness of a particular cause than spending hours and money on a short-term hit. And trying to capitalise on web trends – using the latest app or gizmo popular with youngsters – can have the potentially unfortunate effect of alienating your older audience.

TIPS AND HOW-TO VIDEOS

Tips and How-Tos can be a hugely beneficial addition to a longer form video.

When we are dealing with a subject that is potentially very dry or hard to explain – let's say we are making a science or health-related video that has a lot of experts talking about issues that are hard to grasp – we like to put in a section on tips or 'How to'. Viewers have an automatic, simple reaction to these short clips and for the person on camera it serves a double purpose: it not only humanises them ('Hey! I'm not just an expert in neural misfunction, but I'm a real person just like you and here's a helpful tip that you might like!'), but it also allows them to speak off the cuff and say something that they might normally feel too constricted to say. Many times I have asked an expert to give their own personal top tip and I have seen an immediate change in their body posture and a relaxing of their attitude. It frees them up – and being free on camera is vital – and always makes for a better film.

ARE THE NUMBERS ALWAYS RIGHT?

If you spend any time at all reading about Social Video on websites that give the impression of having some authority, or if you've employed a digital agency to create a social video campaign for you, then you are more than likely going to be hit hard with one thing: stats. These stats are there to please you, to make you feel warm and fuzzy about the product you are going to spend your hard-earned cash on. Usually these stats come in the form of statements such as 'videos will make three times the amount of people come to visit your website'. Or 'search traffic will be increased by 120% if you have a video on your site'. Or 'consumers are 80% more likely to buy after seeing a video on your site'. They try to hit all the bases: from attraction to conversion to loyalty.

Be aware.

I'm not saying these numbers are wrong or deceitful , but I am saying tread carefully before you find yourself leaving a meeting repeating the mantra 'These videos are going to give me an ROI of 500%!' Examine who is telling you, what they are telling you and take a step back to make sure the facts are both watertight as well as applicable to you. And then go and double-check those facts.

MEASURING SUCCESS THE HANDFACE WAY

One of the major problems we see – which I've been at pains to point out above – is marketing departments that fail to understand how to push and promote their video correctly. This can be for a variety of reasons – from flux in the workforce (a person who commissioned a project might have moved on), to having too many projects on the go, to firefighting several other issues.

All of this leads to a lack of focus. And a lack of focus leads to a waste of money.

To combat this, our typical initial walkthrough with a new client will examine everything from 360 degrees – including where they are at now in terms of overall digital marketing, where their competitors are at, who is their digital audience, and what are the expectations of their audience. We look at everything from identifying movers and shakers in their customer base to planning out just what the exact aims of the campaign is going to be (call-to-action/explanation/shareable content etc etc).

Only then do we go away and think about ideas. And once those ideas are solidified and actually made, we're not just going to press send and walk away. The minutiae of following up once an online video has been released – which is still ignored by many, many companies – is key to that piece of content's success.

A FINAL LIST

Some parting random thoughts on the whys and whatnots of video creation and sharing:

1.Tweets that contain an image or a video top Twitter's chart of 'most retweeted'. In other words, the most successful retweets contain an image or a video. This information was made public by Twitter in early 2014 and underlines once again the essential nature of rich media. It's especially the case, as you might expect, with tweets that concern entertainment: an entertainment-based tweet that contains a video is far more likely to be retweeted than one that merely contains a hashtag.

2. Always remember that emotion is the prime driver in video sharing. Particularly happiness. What kind of emotion is your video going to bring to the fore?

3. The age of the large social networks is coming to an end. It's no longer enough to conquer YouTube, Facebook or Twitter. A whole host of new social networks, which each covers a specific area, is going to emerge in the next ten years. From 2013 Vine was just one example. Secret, Whisper, RebelMouse, Facebook's own Paper were just some of the names being discussed as ones to watch in this space in 2015. And as each new best in show arrives, so does another outlet for video.

4. If you are in the public sector, especially a government agency, you have to be extra skilled in your social media use. Your customers are members of the public and they are likely to be a) resistant to your message and b) ahead of you in terms of using social networks. Any mistake is likely to be pounced upon by traditional media, so you really need to tread carefully.

5. Always try to push the envelope in terms of the type of video you might offer. A 'question' video in which your potential customers might record their own answers might yield surprising success. Or a challenge video in which you ask people to record themselves filming an attempt on a specific challenge. Or maybe you can make a supercut that nobody else has thought of? Or think of a spin on a movie trailer or music video that might get attention?

6. Measuring success comes in a number of different ways: from the pure number of views to click-through to ROI. Before you put any video live you need to have an idea of just what kind of success you are looking for, and how you are going to measure it. But remember that standard ideas of what return on investment is and should be may not always apply: a common question when presenting a potential video campaign to the rest of the company is 'What's the ROI?', as if everything should be completely trackable and measurable. While you are seeking some sort of action (passive or active) as a result of your video, there are other commonplace standard activities about which you could ask exactly the same question: networking and attending conferences are acceptable business practices, for example, and how is the ROI measured here?

7. An online video view is worth as much as a TV view. There is an increasingly growing groundswell of opinion that says this is the case, and if so it's a pretty huge statement. I'm not saying it *definitely* is, as I am yet to see absolute proof, but I have a feeling that parity isn't far off.

8. The 21st century is an 'always on' social world. If your ultimate decision-maker is stuck with a late 20th century mindset, you might be in trouble.

9. Measure your competitors in the social space. How many views have their last five videos had? How many Twitter followers do they have, and how has this changed in the last six months? What campaigns have they run and what external impact have they had on the number of followers they have had across all social networks? You need to be on top of what your competitors are doing in the social video space: and once again the tools are there for you to do so.

10. If you have an established fanbase for your product or service, don't be afraid to encourage them. For example, if you launch new products regularly, then consider asking users to send in unboxing videos (where they film themselves unwrapping and reacting to the products inside). If you spot any users making tribute videos, embrace it and encourage them. Anything that makes your community feel just that – a community – will foster loyalty and a return to your service or product. Fans matter, and well-treated fans who feel invested are fans who will be happy to spend.

11. Always remember that most people are able to retain a huge amount of what they see. Visual memory is, typically, extremely strong. So why shouldn't it be *your* video they are remembering?

12. Don't be afraid to change tack in your marketing and distribution plan. If, for example, you want to target a specific network or website with your video and campaign, then check carefully that it is having the desired effect. Even if you get some social buzz about your video and campaign, is this really stacking

up to create conversions or potential new customers? Talk is just that – talk. If you are getting a lot of chatter when what you want is actually conversion, then don't be afraid to take stock and consider changing your course.

13. Consider asking your viewers questions and measuring their responses. It's easy now to put options at the end of a YouTube video, and is an excellent way of measuring just how many viewers are interested enough to reply, as well as what their actual answers are.

14. While 'television' will undoubtedly still exist in 100 years, it is changing. And it is changing fast. The teens of today are, on average, watching 30 minutes of short video clips, compared to 90-120 minutes of television. And that television might not be regularly scheduled TV. It could be on-demand, catch-up, streaming, or just plain old recorded. TV executives have been tearing their hair out for the last 15 years to try and figure out how to capitalise upon this change – and with the range of streaming and on-demand services that are on offer it's fair to say they have done a pretty good job of it. The manner in which people can access TV is undoubtedly the best it has ever been, and the highest quality TV shows of recent times, such as Breaking Bad, Deadwood or Mad Men (and there are plenty more) surpass anything that has been made purely for the internet. But as streaming services grow bigger and bigger and make more programmes like House of Cards or Orange is the New Black, the distinction between TV and other ways of viewing will become increasingly blurry.

15. Be in it for the long haul. In many ways, creating a viral video is akin to creating a Number 1 record: a lot of people are trying to do it, some people have a knack for it, and for others it may take a

while. It's this latter category that is of interest: there are instances of people or companies who have made tens if not hundreds of videos before they have a hit. But think of all of the videos produced in advance of this as preparation: both in learning how to make videos, how to distribute them and creating a body of work. New fans will be delighted to find a resource in your video library, and just like the musician who suddenly is cast into the limelight after years of work, the value of the back catalogue will increase enormously.

15. The speed at which viral videos are shared is increasing, and it's increasing fast. Some reports state that brand videos are receiving between a third and one half of all of their shares in the first three day's of a video's life. This has two implications: firstly, if you're trying to make something go viral you need to hit the ground running, and make sure your distribution strategy is swift. Secondly, there is still plenty of scope for a video to do well some time after it has been released, so think about how you can give it legs so that it can be re-released on different occasions.

16. Look at how much of your marketing time and spend is devoted to social media. Some reports – even in 2016 – are citing that a lot of organisations are putting less than 10% of their marketing spend into social. This is fine if you are a social media naysayer – and there are some solid reasons to still tread carefully and not overemphasise its importance for certain companies – but if your brand or company is doing any form of marketing and people are talking about you socially, then you'd be wise to make sure you are allocating the right amount of time to assess what they are saying, how they are saying it, what you can learn and how you should react.

17. Consider creating a YouTube channel. Especially if you are in a niche that is underserved, or if you are bringing something unique to the niche. You could even do this if you are not creating videos of your own: you could curate a playlist of relevant videos that viewers could come and find.

18. A viral video is not a TV ad. Think about it, and think about all the differences between the two both from a production point of view and on the distribution side of things. Viral videos should be cheaper to make than TV ads. They should also, essentially, distribute themselves through peer-to-peer popularity, and this should also cost significantly less than buying media time during an ad break. Viewers are in a much more active frame of mind when they are engaging with a viral video, compared to the passive way in which they consume television. And TV ads may have different branding, information and messaging aims than viral videos. These are just some of the ways that viral videos and TV ads differ – there are lots more. Don't confuse the two, especially if you are commissioning some for your company.

19. By 2020, the relationship between brands and their audiences will have evolved considerably. It's already started. Successful brands will no longer talk down to their customers: especially in terms of content. Brands need to harness the power of the content that their customers are creating and work *with* them. Customers may well be making content that is way ahead of what brands are doing: the wise brands will recognise this and react accordingly.

THANKS

Firstly, thanks to Lisa, for being there from the start and for putting up with so many midnight edits. And re-edits.

To everyone who kindly agreed to be interviewed for the book.

To all the people who have collaborated with us in commissioning, writing and creating our videos, in particular David Schneider and David Beresford – please check out their amazing company www.thatlot.co.uk for all-round social media brilliance.

To editor-par-excellence Ian Jones who is @biglittlejones on Twitter.

To everyone who has commissioned work from us – we hope you have had fun and will continue to do so.

To Simon James of www.StandardDesigns.co.uk for the artwork.

To Jill Davies, for her super-sub skills.

For more information about us, check out www.handface.co.uk, follow @handfacevideo or email Paul@handface.co.uk

58501158R00130

Made in the USA
Charleston, SC
12 July 2016